# They Sought
# ✻ a Land

# They Sought ❋ a Land

## A Settlement in the Arkansas River Valley 1840–1870

### William Oates Ragsdale

The University of Arkansas Press
Fayetteville ❋ 1997

ISBN: 978-1-55728-498-3 (cloth)
ISBN: 978-1-68226-165-1 (paper)
eISBN: 978-1-61075-423-1

Manufactured in the United States of America

24   23   22   21   20        5   4   3   2   1

*Designed by Liz Lester*

⊗   The paper used in this publication meets the minimum requirements of the American National Standard for Permanence of Paper for Printed Library Materials Z39.48-1984.

*Library of Congress Cataloging-in-Publication Data*

Ragsdale, William Oates, 1915–
    They sought a land : a settlement in the Arkansas River Valley, 1840–1870 / William Oates Ragsdale.
        p.   cm.
    Includes bibliographical references and index.
    ISBN 1-55728-498-9 (alk. paper)
    1. Associate Reformed Synod of the South (1822–1934)—Arkansas—Pope County—History.   2. Pope County (Ark.)—Church history—19th century.
3. Presbyterians—Arkansas—Pope County—History—19th century.   4. Pope County (Arkansas)—History—19th century.   I. Title.
BX8999.A83A4   1997
285'.176732—dc21                                        97-17937
                                                         CIP

*Emma Susan Oates Ragsdale*
*1874–1929*

*They Sought a Land* is dedicated to my mother, Emma Susan Oates Ragsdale. She was of Scots-Irish parentage: her father had come from the Pisgah community in what is now Gaston County, North Carolina; her mother's parents lived in what is now Rockbridge County, Virginia. My mother was born and reared in the Pisgah, Bethany, and Pottsville communities of Pope County, Arkansas.

Emma Susan Oates Ragsdale's life of humble devotion to God was the inspiration to try to learn more about the Scots-Irish who came in covered wagons and began a settlement in the Arkansas River Valley in the early 1840s.

# Acknowledgments

I am deeply indebted to many people who helped in the preparation of *They Sought a Land.*

I am acknowledging by name a few who contributed. Philip Ward Ragsdale, who typed and retyped the manuscript with only a "thank you"; Margaret Oates Goodman, the authority on the Pisgah-Bethany people; Tamara Tidwell, who is becoming an authority; Katie Murdoch at the Pope County, Arkansas, Library; Thomas Morris and the late Robert Elliott, historians and former pastors, respectively, of the Associate Reformed Presbyterian Church at Pottsville, Arkansas, and Pisgah Church at Gastonia, North Carolina; James Kniskern, Jac Miller, and Thomas T. Thomas, who spent innumerable hours writing many helpful suggestions for the manuscript; John and Embry Shoemaker for making available the Scott Collection of Letters; Mona Cowan for furnishing the Ewing Collection of Letters; the office staff of the Pope County circuit and county clerks; Bus Rye, Pope County tax assessor; Geneva Ferguson and W. L. (Cowboy) Ferguson, who furnished background material; James Ragsdale, who assumed many of my home responsibilities; William H. Bowen, who dispensed encouragement all along the way; Daniel F. Littlefield Jr. of the University of Arkansas at Little Rock, and Christopher McCarty, research and editorial assistant, who helped edit the manuscript for publication.

# Contents

# ❋ Chapter 1 ❋

# They Sought a Land

In the fall of 1851, a wagon train consisting of several households gathered near Kings Mountain in Gaston County, North Carolina, preparing to undertake a journey of hundreds of miles to Pope County, Arkansas. The travelers knew a good deal about their destination, for information about its opportunities had come back to their community from its former members who had immigrated to Pope County in the early 1840s. The new adventurers had also sent out a scouting party of their own in 1850, and the move they were about to make was based on that party's report. Just as they were not the first from their community to settle in Pope County, neither would they be the last. However, they were the first mass migration out of their home region during the 1850s and were destined to become founders of a community in Pope County called Pisgah, near present-day Pottsville.

The vast majority of settlers who formed the Pisgah community in Arkansas came from two church communities, and many of those who came from elsewhere, especially Tennessee, had former ties to them: Pisgah in Gaston County, North Carolina, and Bethany in adjoining York County, South Carolina. These were remarkably homogeneous communities, for the most part Scots or Scots-Irish farmers, well established and substantial, whose families had lived for many decades—some nearly a century—in the Carolinas. These Presbyterians, specifically Associate Reformed Presbyterians, from two different congregations, were served by the same minister. The communities were also bound by many ties of family kinship. Some of the families had known each other and had ties before they came to America, for the most part in the eighteenth century. Here, their kinship lines became inextricably mixed as a result of the families' long, close association on the Carolina and other frontiers. Some still mixed Gaelic with their English in conversation well into the nineteenth century and pronounced their English with a decided Scots accent.[1]

The movement leading to settlement in Arkansas had its beginnings in the Pisgah community and later drew on Bethany to swell its numbers. Letters from Pope County to Alexander Weir, a prominent member of the Pisgah community, give clues to the rising interest in Arkansas during the 1840s. Among the early immigrants from Gaston (formerly Lincoln) County, North Carolina, were John Willson, Moses Wilson, and James A. and Martina Stenson Bradley. Though Moses Wilson has been said to be perhaps the first of these to emigrate,[2] all were in North Carolina in 1840 but were settled and making crops in Arkansas by 1842. These early arrivals settled in what became known as Bradley's Cove or simply "the Cove," a recess in Crow Mountain, forming a basin about three miles long and two miles wide, east of present-day Russellville. The Cove lies about three miles north of the site that the large party of settlers who began immigrating in 1851 would select for a church. The first Carolinians to settle in the area were so well pleased with the land that they began early trying to entice their friend Weir and others to join them.

John Willson apparently moved to Pope County in 1841, for by 1842 he had cleared twenty acres and had put in a crop. On April 25, he wrote Weir about his prospects in language that suggests that this was his first crop season in the west. He thought that the country would produce good corn, wheat, and cotton, and he hoped to have four hundred bushels of wheat off his place. Though there were patches of land that were not well watered, he believed the watercourses ran all summer. The water was as cold and clear in Arkansas as it was back home. Willson told Weir that the grass was knee high all over the woods. He speculated that if cattle in North Carolina knew about such grass they would all join him in Arkansas. Wild game abounded. He had killed four old bucks and so many turkeys he lost count. He saw a bear, but when it saw him, it ran and he did not get a shot. Two big panthers had been killed on "This Big Mountain" (apparently Crow Mountain), one of which was seven feet long. Willson urged Weir to join him soon. Good land could be bought for $1.25 an acre. The sooner Weir came the better, for land was being taken up fast. John Willson also sent news of eighteen-year-old Moses Wilson, who had improved a place and was preparing to put up a house. Wilson was anticipating word that others, perhaps his family, were preparing to move to Arkansas. "He has got no Word from them yet," wrote

John, "and he is very oneasy to know if tha are coming and if tha are he says that he will go back and help them out."[3]

To John Willson's letter, Moses penned a note on April 30. Moses, who may have gone west with James and Martina Bradley, was boarding with them. He had left Mr. Shinn's "on the count of the money," he said. He had four acres of land cleared and planned to put up a log house shortly, and he had bought a cow and a calf. Like John, Moses thought it would be a "good noshing" for Alexander Weir to bring his family to Arkansas. He asked Weir to let Samuel Wilson read his note.[4]

What relationship Moses bore to John, if any, is unknown. Little is known about the latter, but Moses was the son of Thomas and Jane Whitesides Wilson. His grandparents, Samuel and Mary Wilson, and their five children, including Thomas, had immigrated from Belfast to Charleston in 1767, eventually settling in the section of Gaston County known as Crowder's Mountain. When Thomas Wilson and Jane Whitesides married, they settled near Pisgah Church.[5]

James (1798–1870) and Martina Bradley (1801–1895), with whom Moses Wilson had boarded, left North Carolina on May 13, 1842, with their children John M., Samuel S., Sidney A., Jemima, and Melvin R. The Bradleys were cousins, he the son of John M. and Jenny Williams Bradley and she the daughter of George and Esther Bradley Stinson. Their great-grandparents had immigrated from Wales and England, respectively, and had married in North Carolina in 1742. James A. and Martina Bradley were apparently members of the Pisgah Church, for Bradley was listed as one of the early emigrants from that community to Arkansas. The Bradleys had settled in "a cove a mong the mountiens," where by the summer of 1842, they had bought "a small improvement of land with four or five acres of land cleared."[6]

On September 15 he, like Willson, reported his impressions of the country to Weir. Bradley had dug a well and had opened new fields. The corn he raised was as good as any he had grown on Crowder's Creek back in North Carolina. He hoped to have eight barrels of corn to the acre. "Beat that on your upland if you can," he wrote. He had one and one-half acres of turnips. Wheat grew well, and cotton and tobacco could also be raised. The soil was sandy, easy to work, and produced well. Livestock lived on the range all year. "I can show you grass in this cove that you cant see a deer run through only now and then," he wrote. Bradley had been told there were large steers in the Cove that had never tasted corn. There were good springs on the place. Their animals had running water in the creek all summer. Bradley confirmed Willson's assertion about wildlife. "East Mountain" was nearby and "was several miles across a pine range." Bradley thought that panthers, bears, wolves, and all kinds of game would make their home there for a long time to come. As to snakes, he had not seen as many as he had back in Lincoln County. There were times he could walk all day and not see one.[7]

"I am pretty well satisfied with my move taking every thing into consideration," he said. The country was healthy. Though the family had suffered some illness, taken all around, he had been "hartier" that summer than in many years. Bradley also thought the people to be "very sivel kind and obliging about as good neighbors as anywhere." There were also "conveniences" in their location. Their home was only six miles from a steamboat landing. Nine miles from the Bradley place was a sawmill that sawed some timber. Sixteen miles away was a steam mill that sawed a great deal more. "But the maul and weg is saw mill for a good many the ax Jack plane and Jointer," he wrote.[8]

Times were hard in Pope County, just as they were elsewhere, but Bradley did not think that should stop those who contemplated joining him. "People have to labour under dificulties in new setelments," he said. "I think if I had [a] start made I could liv easier here a good deal than where I left. I had rather be in a fresh new country than in Lincoln." Martina sent a message to Weir's wife: "Martyne says to tell mary that she had beter come out here and have good water in the yard than carey it up the big hill when she [Martina] might draw 6 loads while she can carey one and with less slavery."[9]

Thus Bradley encouraged others from his former North Carolina neighborhood to come. "If any of my old neighbours could reconsile themselvs to Arkinsaw I would be glad to see them here I think youn[g] men would do well to ride out and see for them selvs what will suite one will not sute all so let all look for them selvs I think there is better pleases than old lincoln."[10]

The correspondence from Willson and Bradley to Weir and others probably helped spread the word about Pope County to the people of Lincoln County. Weir's wife, Mary Oates Weir, had ties to a number of families besides Oates in the Pisgah community, including Dickey, Falls, and Ferguson, who would ultimately make their way to Pope County. Moses Wilson's sister and her husband, James Whitesides, would also make the move. But the early correspondence indicates that the new Pope County residents kept in touch with others from their old neighborhood whom Weir knew: James McNair, James H. White, and John Gamble. As they did with Weir, they asked these friends to pass word of them among their old neighbors. During the early 1840s, a number of their mutual acquaintances left Lincoln County and went to Pope County: Caleb Kizer, Robert Clark, Jacob and Joseph Mendenhall, D. Clemmer, and Samuel M. Robinson. Also in Pope County were Joshua Hearne and James Wells, who arrived about the same time as Bradley. Some of these joined the army during the Mexican War and did not return. Others moved elsewhere. Some apparently returned to North Carolina.[11] In 1846 Bradley wrote to Weir: "A good deal of stir about moveing some to one place and some to another a grate many for taxis [Texas] I say to none come nor to any stay because one place will not suit all what mite please me not please a nother let all Juge for them selves."[12]

Though few of the early Lincoln County immigrants appear to have stayed in Pope County, their connection to Alexander Weir was significant in laying the groundwork for the great migrations in the 1850s. Of those who remained, only Moses Wilson and James A. Bradley are known to have had ties to the Pisgah Church, which formed the nucleus for the covered-wagon migrations of the fifties. By the late 1840s a large number of the congregation was apparently contemplating a move to Arkansas.

Many of the men who had some interest in taking their families to Arkansas were older men. For their own sake, they had no reason for moving, for they were financially well fixed for the time. Their interest in seeking a land on the western frontier was to improve the lot of their children. Thus wrote a historian of the Pisgah Church in North Carolina: "While the motive which prompted the move to Arkansas can be stated definitely as economic, it can be stated with equal assurance that the establishment of a church was a part of the original plan."[13] This statement reflects the central role that the Associate Reformed Presbyterian Church, along with the predominantly Scots-Irish origin and a web of family connections, played in forming the tightly knit communities at Pisgah and Bethany, which the Carolinians would replicate at Pisgah in Pope County during the 1850s. Migration had been a part of their history for a century and a half; they were willing to move again to achieve their goals.

The Associate Reformed Presbyterians at Pisgah and Bethany had inherited a long history, dating from the seventeenth century, of continuing the Protestant reformation, insisting on a strict adherence to church principles, resisting innovations in church government or practice, and maintaining a clear separation between the civil state and the church in America, although they did not oppose an establishment principle absolutely. They did, however, uphold the prerogatives of the church to decide its doctrines, worship, and discipline. Though their church was formed by a union of the Associate Presbyterian Church and the Reformed Presbyterian Church, they refused to distinguish themselves from the Scottish Church or from each other in their adherence to the doctrinal symbols of the church: the Westminster Confession of Faith and the Larger Catechism and Shorter Catechism. Their separate organizations resulted, rather, from the actions of eighteenth-century Seceders and Covenanters, whose consciences led them to struggle against corrupt government or practice in the mother church.

The Associate Presbytery was formed in 1733 near Kinross, Scotland, composed of ministers Ebenezer Erskine, James Fisher, William Wilson, and Alexander Moncrieff. Their followers were known as Seceders because of their secession from the Church of Scotland as a result of their opposition to vestiges of the Episcopal form of government, imposed on the church from 1661 to 1689, that remained in the eighteenth-century church. It had also admitted some who were not Calvinistic in their doctrinal beliefs but were in reality Arminians and Socinians. And the practice of patronage in the appointment of ministers had continued since the days of the Roman Catholic Church. Erskine and his associates were censured by the general assembly of the Church of Scotland for preaching against patronage and then suspended from the ministry. Thus they seceded and formed the Associate Presbytery of Scotland and were joined in 1737 by the Reverends Ralph Erskine and Thomas Mair. In 1740, Erskine and his associates were deposed by the general assembly. A synod, including three Presbyteries and twenty-six ministers, was organized in 1744, but the following year the synod split in a controversy over an oath to be sworn by the freemen or burghers in the towns. Both groups, known as the burghers and anti-burghers, claimed title to the Associate Synod. In later years, when members of both groups immigrated to America, the exigencies of frontier life resulted in their worship in the same congregations.[14]

The Reformed Presbyterian Church was founded in 1743 when the Reverends John McMillan and Thomas Nairn formed the Reformed Presbytery. Known as Covenanters, the Reformed Presbyterians were the descendants or followers of those who had been persecuted or martyred because they had refused to recognize the supremacy of the crown over the church. The Covenanters had bound themselves in the National Covenant (1638) and the expanded Solemn League and Covenant (1643) to carry forward and defend the Reformed religion unto death, some signing the documents with their own blood. When Episcopal services were imposed upon the churches in Scotland, they resisted with arms and were defeated at Bothwell Bridge in 1679. Then began a period of persecution and martyrdom. Persecution was extreme in the years 1684 to 1688, which became known in Covenanter history as "the killing time." The persecutions came to an end with the restoration of Presbyterianism in 1690.

With the restoration, some Covenanters joined the reorganized church. The few who remained outstanding did so because the religious settlement did not recognize the Solemn League and Covenant and recognized the supremacy of the crown over the church. In 1690, however, these, too, rejoined the national church, and the Covenanters had no minister for the next sixteen years. They became known as the Society People, for they organized into praying societies, meeting for religious worship and caring for the spiritual needs of one another. Then the Reverend John McMillan, ejected from the established church for antigovernment sentiments, accepted their call for a minister and for more than thirty years was their only ordained minister. The Reverend Thomas Nairn, who came to accept their views on civil government, came to them from the Associate Presbytery and, with McMillan, formed the Reformed Presbytery. Their principles included adherence to the Westminster Confession of Faith and the Catechisms, the divine right of Presbytery, and the singing of the Psalms as their form of praise. In addition, they refused to recognize any political institution that would exert ecclesiastical authority over them. In later years, on the American frontier, this fierce independence continued to grow and their practice of forming praying societies served them well in their scattered settlements while they petitioned for ministers.

Covenanters began to arrive in America by 1685, and their numbers increased during the succeeding decades, primarily in New England, New Jersey, Pennsylvania, and, later, South Carolina. From the time of their arrival until the early 1750s the Reformed Presbyterians had organized themselves into societies and had no minister until 1752. The Reformed Presbyterian Presbytery was organized in Pennsylvania in 1774. Associates came also, settling in the same colonies as the Covenanters and in Virginia and by 1753 were in America in such numbers as to organize the Associate Presbytery of Pennsylvania, followed by the Presbytery of New York in 1776. These organizations resulted from the Associate and Reformed Presbyterians immigration of Scots and Scots-Irish settlers to the frontiers. Extensive immigration occurred to the south, particularly the Carolinas, from Scotland, Ireland, where many had fled to escape persecution, and from the northern colonies, especially Pennsylvania.[15]

Against this broad historical backdrop, communities such as Pisgah in North Carolina and Bethany in South Carolina developed and their churches were established. The people who made up these churches had been part of the great migration of Scots and Scots-Irish to the Carolinas after 1735. By 1750 they had established "a broad band of settlements," as one writer put it, "extending from the sandhills to the mountains." They were all Presbyterians, primarily Scottish Presbyterians and Associate Presbyterians, who joined in forming churches. By 1782, it was estimated that more than fifty societies, both Associate and Reformed, had organized south of the James River, and by 1790 Presbyterians of all types worshiped together in the North Carolina and South Carolina border region of Lincoln and York counties at Long Creek, Beersheba, Goshen, and Bethel.[16]

These Presbyterians carried with them to the American frontier a fierce sense of independence that had led their ancestors to take up arms against the crown or to secede from the authority of the general assembly of the Scottish Church for matters of conscience, though they meant to remain "associated" with the true Church of Scotland. The Westminster Confession told them, "God alone is lord of the conscience, and hath left it free from the doctrines and commandments of men which are in anything contrary to his word, or beside it, in matters of faith or worship." Their antagonism to the English crown had grown through their long history of resistance to its attempts at ecclesiastical authority by the Act of Uniformity (1662), the Conventicle Act (1664), and the "killing time." The economic policies of the colonial governments reminded them of the economic restrictions Parliament placed on them in Ulster, where many had gone to escape persecution. Their collective historical consciousness practically assured the participation of the Scots-Irish on the patriot side of the American Revolution.

So it was with the Scots-Irish who populated the Carolina upland regions where the Pisgah and Bethany communities would later be established. The war came literally to their doors. The battle of Kings Mountain, fought in 1780 in their midst, was one of the most decisive battles of the southern campaign. Except for about one hundred British soldiers, the battle was between volunteers from the Carolinas, Virginia, Georgia, and what is now east Tennessee. Led by Maj. Patrick Ferguson, the loyalists were mainly from the lowlands and piedmont and the patriots from the uplands. By the time of the revolution, an estimated nine hundred thousand of the colonies' estimated three million population were Scots and Scots-Irish, whose role in the war has been well documented. So conspicuous was their presence that George III was alleged to have called it "a Presbyterian rebellion." At Kings Mountain, most of the patriot volunteers came from Presbyterian settlements, and five of the six colonels in command were Presbyterian elders. Pisgah and Bethany, because of their proximity to the battle site, supplied a large number of volunteers. Among those who would move from those communities to Arkansas in the 1850s was a number who had fathers and grandfathers who were Kings Mountain veterans.[17]

In 1782 a majority of the Presbyteries of the Associate and Reformed groups in America merged to form the Associate Reformed Presbyterian Church. During the twenty years thereafter the church flourished, in part because of the uniformity of their beliefs. Both adhered to the Westminster standards and used the Psalms as their form of praise. In 1799 they revised the Confession of Faith regarding the civil magistrate to fit the new political realities of America and published it with the Catechisms as *The Constitution and Standards of the Associate Reformed Church in North America,* which went unchanged into the twentieth century. By 1803 the Associate Reformed Church consisted of four synods: the Synod of New York, the Synod of Pennsylvania, the Synod of Scioto, and the Synod of the Carolinas. This latter, organized in 1803, reflected the growing strength of the denomination in the south.

Pisgah Church was established as the result of a controversy that erupted after 1789 over the introduction of Watts' Hymns to the worship of the Presbyterian Church. Some members of the congregations at Beersheba in South Carolina and Long Creek in North Carolina adhered to the Psalms and considered the hymns "uninspired praise." Sometime before 1795, perhaps in 1793, they withdrew, formed the Old Kings Mountain Church on the south slope of Kings Mountain, and applied to the Associate Reformed Presbytery of the Carolinas for a minister.[18] Robert Elliott, historian of Pisgah, wrote: "The names of those families from both Beersheba and Long Creek that formed the nucleus of the Old Kings Mountain Church were: William McElwee, Sr. (ruling Elder at Beersheba) and his sons John McElwee and William McElwee, William Henry, Alexander Henry, James Henry, James Crawford, William Crawford, Francis Rea, James Dunn, Joseph Carroll, John Oates, James Blackwood, probably also the Sarvices, Falls, Fergursons, Beatties, and Wilsons."[19] A number of these same families would later supply settlers to build the Pisgah community in Arkansas. For eighteen months to two years, the church was supplied by Associate Reformed Church licentiate William Dixon.

In 1796, the church divided by mutual consent into two congregations, forming Pisgah and Bethany. Preaching began at a stand at Bethany, farther to the south, apparently for the convenience of the people on the south side of Kings Mountain. Bethany was organized in 1797 with William McElwee Sr., Samuel Leslie, James Crawford, and Alexander Henry as elders. The people on the north side of the mountain built a church at Pisgah, about four miles east of the village of Kings Mountain. The Reverend William Dixon was ordained and installed and supplied both churches as well as Sharon in York County, South Carolina, from their founding until 1828. During his ministry, Dixon took his congregations out of the Associate Reformed Church and, with the Reverends Peter McMillan and John Cree, formed the Associate Presbytery of the Carolinas. In 1833, several of the congregations asked for readmission to the Associate Reformed Presbyterian Church. At the union meeting in early 1833, representing Pisgah was John Falls and representing Bethany was John McElwee. The union was completed that summer, and the two congregations thereafter remained in the Associate Reformed Presbyterian Church.[20]

By the late 1840s the countryside around Pisgah and Bethany, which had been raw and isolated when the Scots-Irish settlers occupied it after defeat of the Cherokees in 1761, had become more densely populated, the soil had become depleted, and less good arable land was available for the oncoming generations. There had already been migrations from the Pisgah community to Tennessee and other states, where societies or Associate Reformed Presbyterian churches had been established. Some of the older, stalwart members of the Pisgah congregation gave in to the invitations from former neighbors who had gone west and, for the sake of their children, began to lay plans to give up the comfort and prosperity they enjoyed in North Carolina and seek a land where their posterity could enjoy better economic prospects. Those plans would lead to the mass migrations from Pisgah and Bethany to Pope County, Arkansas, during the next few years. The emigrants would be joined by friends and relatives from elsewhere, especially some who had gone earlier to Tennessee. Together they would build a new Pisgah community near present-day Pottsville. By 1860 their community would be remarkable in comparison to the county or the state in general, not only because of religious devotion among its members but also because of its economic success.

# ❋ Chapter 2 ❋

# The First Migrations, 1850-1852

By 1850, in the Pisgah community in North Carolina and the Bethany community in South Carolina, there had been years of discussion about a move to the west. Interest in migration to Arkansas had probably spread through letters to relatives in Tennessee, who had moved there from Pisgah some years earlier, and through the earlier migration to Arkansas of young men such as John Willson and Moses Wilson and families such as that of James A. and Martina Bradley. The move in the offing by the Pisgah, Bethany, and Tennessee groups was in some respects a continuation of that earlier migration to make a settlement in Arkansas, and the movement became what Neill Bell has called a "planned group affair."[1] Though their motive was economic, the emigrants were also concerned about "forming a congregation, worshipping together and having the Gospel preached among them."[2] Thus with these plans began a series of moves that spanned most of the 1850s, but those in 1851 and 1852 were the most important, not simply because they were the first major migrations but because they would result in the establishment of the first Associate Reformed Presbyterian Church west of the Mississippi.

The people of Bethany and Pisgah were familiar with the biblical story of Joshua sending out spies to look over the land and people of the Promised Land. Though they would not send spies, they would send out parties to assess Arkansas as a possible place to establish a colony. Whether, as rumors indicated, John Oates IV and Andrew Nael Falls had journeyed to Arkansas in the 1840s, they became the prime movers in the venture, Falls becoming what might be considered an enthusiastic booster for migration and settlement. Still, there was need for caution, and a plan was devised, perhaps at Oates's request, to send a small advance party to Arkansas, seeking out the best place for settlement, if settlement was feasible.

This party, which left Gaston County, North Carolina, in the fall of 1850, consisted of William Oates Jr. (1823–1877) and John M. Ferguson;

their wives, Rosa Falls Ferguson and Frances (Fannie) Falls Oates (1825–1895), who were sisters; and Joseph D. Oates, who was single.[3] With William and Fannie Oates were their children John, Sarah, and William. They had reached Mississippi by early December, when on the fourth, Rosa Ferguson bore a son, whom she and John named William O. The party crossed the Mississippi River at Memphis and stopped in Montgomery County near Hot Springs, where they established a base for the following year.[4]

Their travel route through Arkansas was one that others who followed would take. From Memphis, the wagon road went west through Marion to St. Francisville on the west side of the St. Francis River. This segment of the road crossed two swamps at the Blackfish River and St. Francis River. From St. Francisville, the road angled southwest toward Little Rock, across the swamps in the Cache and White River bottoms. On the north side of the Big Meto, the road intersected others from Des Arc to the north, Clarendon to the southeast, and Cadron to the northwest. Travelers to Pope County could take the road to Cadron or go south to the Arkansas River opposite Little Rock, where another road went northwest to Cadron, Lewisburg, Remove, and Norristown. From Little Rock, a road went southwest to Hot Springs and Sulphur Springs in Montgomery County.

The arrival of more North Carolinians was not surprising to Montgomery County residents. During the previous year, emigrants from North Carolina and Georgia had made a "very considerable addition" to the county's population. Local observers believed that people from those regions found the area pleasing because its uplands were on about the same latitude as those they had left and because the climate was healthy. In the fall of 1850, Montgomery Countians were expecting another large migration from the same states.[5] For the advance party from Gaston County, however, the stop to search for farm land was not necessarily permanent, for their purpose was to look also at the land in Pope County that might be suitable for settlement. Using Montgomery County as a base, early in 1851 some members of the advance party apparently went on to Pope County to carry out their mission.

They found Pope County less isolated than Montgomery and rapidly developing because it was on the main travel route through Arkansas to Fort Smith, which had become a major center for forming up wagon trains of emigrants headed for the gold fields of California. In 1850 Pope County had a population of 4,231 whites, who held 479 slaves.[6] The young explorers would have found a trade center at Norristown, south of present-day Russellville, settled in 1829 by Samuel Norris of Philadelphia. Boats loaded and unloaded passengers and cargo there. People came from as far away as the Boston Mountains to get provisions when boats could not go farther upstream. Norristown was the county seat from 1834 to 1842 and at its height had a population of three to four hundred people. The military road, cut between Fort Smith and Little Rock in 1845, ran through Norristown, making once-a-week postal service available from Little Rock. The explorers also probably looked over Dover, the county seat, and Galley, south of present-day Pottsville on the river, settled by the Cherokees under the leadership of John Jolly in 1817 but was abandoned in 1828 when the Cherokees exchanged land in Arkansas for land west of the territorial boundary. Galley became known as Galley Rock, which was incorporated in 1837. The higher hills at Galley Rock were close to the Arkansas River, the high ground furnishing a boat landing. Residing in Galley Rock Township were the families of Lincoln Countians James Bradley, Moses Wilson, and John Willson, who had lived in Arkansas almost ten years. There were other Carolinians that John Ferguson and the Oates family may have contacted for advice: William W. Rankin, who had come to the state in 1832, and Darling Love, who had come from Cabarras County, North Carolina, in 1839. James Wells had come from their own Lincoln County and settled in Holly Bend. Joshua Hearne, also from Lincoln County, was there, as was Thomas J. Dare of South Carolina.

After the advance party from Gaston County had made a careful study of both Montgomery and Pope counties, they were to regroup with those that followed at the preferable one.[7] Time came for them to weigh the prospects of the two sites. In Pope County, they could see the possibilities for farming in not only the bottoms but on the uplands as well. Still, they would learn the perils of farming and living in the Arkansas River bottoms. There were swampy places that were breeding grounds for mosquitoes and "fevers." Call it malaria, swamp, or typhoid fever—all were diseases found not only in the bottoms but in the uplands around Galley Rock.

Still, this countryside had more appeal than that in Montgomery County. There is evidence that they were afraid of "volcanic disturbances" in the Hot Springs region, causing them to reject it for a permanent location.[8] But there were probably other factors. For one, Montgomery County may have been too lawless for a group of devout Associate

Reformed Presbyterians. The national debate over the Compromise of 1850 had resulted in much popular attention to activities of abolitionists in the south. Stories abounded about organized rings of slave stealers, whose purpose was to run slaves off to the north. In the spring of 1850, Montgomery County citizens discovered what they thought was a connection between a local citizen and a slave-stealing ring whose influence reached from Missouri to Louisiana. More than a hundred of the citizenry organized as regulators, shooting up suspects, threatening lynching, defying the sheriff, and shutting down the circuit court for a time. Montgomery County was still trying to overcome its image of anarchy in the state press during the fall of 1850, shortly before the advance party arrived. One local observer commented that the excitement caused by the regulators had died down. "I am proud," he said, "to believe that at this time a more industrious, moral and religious community than this county affords can not be found in this State."[9] Still, to a group just arriving and looking to settlement, the accounts of the events of the previous spring must have seemed most unsettling.

The advance party reported to the people of Pisgah and Bethany that the Arkansas River Valley was a good place for settlement. They were a vanguard, a commencement, and now they must await action by the home folks. In the meantime, they continued to make their camp in Montgomery County, awaiting the arrival of others.

A momentous decision would be made back in the Carolinas. The hour that a number in the community had been working for for years had come. Families now had to make decisions about selling farms and other properties, and selecting what of their furniture to take in covered wagons to Arkansas. Sixty-five-year-old John Oates IV (1786–1858), for instance, had long anticipated a settlement in Arkansas. If not the leader in this movement, his role in it was large. Now he must make a crucial decision. Should he pull up stakes and move?

Oates was a life-long resident of the Pisgah community. He descended from John Oates and Frances Reid Oates, who emigrated from Northern Ireland in 1734 and settled first in Pennsylvania. His father, John Oates III, migrated to North Carolina and built a house on the Upper Fork of Crowder's Creek in 1780, not far from where the Pisgah Church was later established. He married Mary Henry Blackwood, a native of County Tyrone, Ireland, in 1782 and reared his family. After the death of this couple in 1830 and 1842, respectively, John IV took possession of the farm and was living there in 1851.[10] His farm, mill, slaves, gold, and other material things made him "well off" by the standards of the day. He was close to his beloved Pisgah Church in which he served as an elder. Was the proposed move to Arkansas one that would haunt him in his last years? Could he make the transition to living on a western frontier?

The other side of the question was what would be most beneficial to his children: eight sons and three daughters. Two of his sons were below the age of ten, while some of his children were married with children of their own. They were living on land that one former Lincoln Countian, James A. Bradley, had described as "wore out." At this time, it appeared that all of Oates's children would make their living off the land, except one son, Monroe, who was preparing for the ministry at Erskine College at Due West, South Carolina. Arkansas was well known for cheap land, some of it fertile. Putting his own comfort aside, he faced the question: Would the old "wore out" land or the Arkansas land offer the better opportunity for his children? He might well have asked the same questions about his nieces and nephews, the children of William and Margaret Oates and Betsy and John Falls.

Another issue that concerned the Oates family and others of the religious community who were contemplating a move was the priority of setting up a church in the new land. They would carry the banner of Zion to the west. The land they sought might not be the new Jerusalem, but it was a land of promise. John Oates IV was decisive. Calvin Grier Oates, who was nine years old at the time, later in life said of his father: "In 1851, he sold his farm and mill and started to Arkansas."[11]

After such a lapse of time, it is difficult to determine the number and identity of those who made up this first large contingent of covered-wagon emigrants from the Pisgah and Bethany communities. One estimate puts the number at approximately seventy-five.[12] Calvin Grier Oates and his brother Monroe listed the following among those who made up the train: James S. and Catherine Wilson Whitesides (1821–1872) and children Thomas, William, and Sarah; Andrew N. (1815–1900) and Margaret Quinn Falls (1817–1879) and children James, Elizabeth, Ebenezer, and George; William Sr. (1791–1866) and Margaret Dickey Oates (1789–1870); their son John (1813–1859) and his wife, Eliza Reed Oates, and children Newton, John, Martha, Thomas, Eliza R., and Margaret; their son

Thomas M. and his wife, Nancy Ann Blackwood Oates; their daughter Emily and her husband, Thomas Warren Ferguson, and children John M., Mary E., and William; John Oates IV; his daughter Margaret Oates Bigham (1825–1871) and her daughter Nancy; and his sons James A., Calvin G., and Samuel W. Oates. Also in the party was James and Ann Falls Quinn (1820–1894).[13]

Another person who came with the group in 1851 was Dr. Ebenezer E. Boyce. Boyce was prepared for college at the renowned Union Academy of Sardis Church in North Carolina under Dr. R. C. Grier. After Union Academy, he attended Jefferson College in Pennsylvania, and after a full course at Erskine Seminary, he became a probationer for the First Presbytery on November 11, 1846. On June 28, 1849, he was ordained and installed pastor of Bethany Church, York County, South Carolina, and Pisgah, Gaston County, North Carolina.[14] The presence of Dr. Boyce was significant. The worship services he provided on the Lord's Day were no doubt an inspiring experience for all and encouraged and strengthened the people on their journey. Later, when Boyce returned to North Carolina to his Bethany-Pisgah pastorate, he would prove a great assistance to the Arkansas people. In the church courts, he would help secure ministers for the church the people would organize at Pisgah in Pope County.

How many slaves were in this party is uncertain. A. N. Falls had four slaves in 1850, but only one in 1852; John Oates and Thomas M. Oates had one each; Thomas W. Ferguson had three in 1850, but none in 1852; John Oates IV had eleven; and James Quinn Falls had nine in 1850, but only three in 1852.[15] These figures reflect the kind of farmers the Pisgah settlers typically were: yeoman farmers, not plantation owners. While one might assume that they brought most, if not all, of their slaves with them, the decline in the number of slaves owned by some when they first appear on Pope County tax rolls remains unexplained.

The covered-wagon settlers who made the trek in 1851 took a route that subsequent emigrants would approximately follow. Starting near present-day Gastonia, North Carolina, they traveled southeast through Greenville, South Carolina, on to Decatur, Georgia, apparently their farthest point south, where they turned northwest to Rome, Georgia, thus skirting the lower reaches of the Smoky Mountains in northwest Georgia and northeast Alabama. Turning northwest, they traveled toward the Alabama Tennessee line and then went west toward Memphis. They stopped in

Wayne County, Tennessee, to visit friends and relatives who had moved there from their community twenty years earlier.[16]

From Memphis, the 1851 group made the next leg of their journey by water. The lowlands west of Memphis were impassable in wagons. Thus they went by boat down the Mississippi to the mouth of the White River and up the White to what is now Prairie County, where they started west by wagon once more. The party split, one group going through Little Rock to Montgomery County to visit the advance scouting party and the rest going directly to Pope County. The wagon train was some three months on the road, traveling about twenty miles a day. The emigrants did not travel on Sunday but stopped instead to hold religious services.[17]

They added their numbers to a community in which there were people they already knew: James Bradley's family and those of John Willson and Moses Wilson, the latter a brother of Catherine Wilson Whitesides. They might also have known the Wells and Hearne families, formerly of Lincoln County. In addition to the Pisgah immigrants, the new arrivals in the community included Peter (1808–1886) and Anna Berry Hoffman (1810–1875) and their family, German Lutherans who also came from Gaston County and relocated among the Pisgah settlers in Pope County. The year before he left North Carolina, Hoffman owned eleven slaves. How many of these he took to the west is uncertain, but he most likely brought some, for he remained a slave keeper in Pope County. The Hoffmans apparently left North Carolina at about the same time as the Oates party, for they brought with them a letter from their church dated September 28, 1851. Because there was no Lutheran church at their new location, Hoffman joined no church. However, he was considered an honorable man of whom it was said that "the vilest tramp never asked for bread and asked in vain."[18] Though not members of the religious community, the Hoffmans entered the social and economic life of the Pisgah settlers, with whose children some of their grandchildren intermarried.

These families had gone a long distance, mostly in search of land, which they began to buy immediately. Andrew N. Falls, Peter Hoffman, and James Quinn bought land in December 1851. Also, early in 1852, members of the advance scouting party, and those who had stopped to see them, went on to Pope County, where William Oates Sr. and John Oates IV immediately bought land.[19] "They settled near together," Monroe Oates would later write of his father and his party, "that they might be helpers one of another and with a view as soon as practicable of forming a congregation, and worshipping together, and having the Gospel preached among them."[20] On their new land, the settlers faced challenges of felling trees to build their homes and barns, but most bought tracts containing some improved land so that by the spring of 1852 they were ready to begin farming. Along with other pioneers their spirits were lifted by the opportunities before them. Though not the first to come, the emigrants of 1851 were a harbinger of many others of their relatives and friends who would come in large numbers seeking land until the late 1850s.

Late in the season in 1852, the covered wagons rolled again in the second great migration from the Carolinas to Pope County. John Falls Sr. (1786–1855) was the senior member of the caravan, among whom were his wife, Betsy Oates Falls (1796–1857); their daughter Margaret (1817–1879), widow of Ellison Falls, and her children; John Falls Jr.; Robert (1814–1860) and Mary Falls Ferguson and their children; Newton and Jane Falls Hays; and Samuel Blackwood. There were slaves in this party as well. How many is uncertain, though John Falls alone had fifteen in 1850. Robert A. Ferguson was also a slave owner.[21]

Ferguson was a good person to have on the trip. He had "gained great proficiency in his studies under the tutelage of Rev. Isaac Grier" and had taught school. He had studied mechanical engineering "in a crude way" and was later a millwright.[22] On the rough wilderness roads the group traveled in their carryalls—two- and four-horse wagons—constant attention needed to be paid not only to the animals but also to the condition of the vehicles.

The party went by Greenville, South Carolina, and Decatur and Rome, Georgia, as the group before them had done, and on to Memphis. There, the party ran into real trouble. Because it was so late in the season, the roads in the Mississippi bottoms were impassable. Thus they boarded the mail boat *Ironton,* went down the Mississippi to the White River, and then up the White to Rock Roe Lake. The weather was terrible. It was so foggy that the pilot could not keep to the channel of the river at night. In these conditions cholera fastened on members of the party. Isabella, daughter of Robert and Mary Ferguson, started vomiting before they left the boat. They stopped on the edge of the Grand Prairie for about a week. Isabella, Samuel Blackwood, and a slave Jude, and perhaps other slaves, died and were buried there. The party proceeded with heavy hearts to Pope County, the sickness still with them.[23]

Meanwhile, death had stalked their friends and family there. Thirty-five-year-old Thomas W. Ferguson, who had arrived with the first group in 1851, was ailing. On September 9, describing himself as "being in a week state of health," he signed a will, leaving his property to his wife, Emily Oates Ferguson.[24] Ferguson descended from substantial Scots stock. His grandfather had settled on the slope of Kings Mountain, North Carolina, on the head of a branch of Crowder's Creek before the Revolution. At the outbreak of the war, he volunteered and served with distinction under General Greene, participating in the battle of Kings Mountain. Before Thomas Ferguson left North Carolina, he owned six hundred acres. In Arkansas, he had quickly reestablished himself. His home was on a tract containing one hundred eighty acres, and he owned forty more in the Arkansas River bottoms. He had amassed farming utensils, household furniture, cattle, hogs, and a horse and had crops of corn, wheat, and oats. Ferguson died on September 13 and was buried in the Cove Cemetery.[25]

Then death struck other families in the new settlement. John Jr. and Eliza Reed Oates lost their son William N. on October 20 and son Alexander D. on November 7. On December 27, George Adams, five-year-old son of Andrew N. and Margaret Quinn Falls, died. Upon his death, his father composed the following elegy:

> We lay thee in thy grave
> To rest beneath the sod
> We give thee up in silent prayer
> Thine infant soul to God.
>
> Dear Shepherd keep this lamb
> Within thy fond embrace
> And in the mansions of Thy rest
> May we behold his face.[26]

Because the Pisgah settlers had not yet established their church, these members were also buried in the Cove Cemetery.

Upon arrival of the Falls caravan in 1852, the families who were already established were quick to minister to weary travelers' needs. However, for all the tender care, the family of Robert A. Ferguson lost their eight-year-old son, Thomas J. Slaves Charles and Roxan also died. A. N. Falls reported these three died at "Uncle John Oats home." He also reported that his sister Margaret Falls and her youngest child had the same disease, but both recovered. The doctor pronounced the disease "cholery." However, it did not spread in the valley. John Falls Sr., leader of the second migration, was sustained by his faith during these difficult times. He came out of a background that interpreted the Scriptures through the lens of the Westminster Confession of Faith and the Catechisms. This was a Providence of God—even though a sorrowful and mysterious one. Falls did not question the sovereignty of God. His son, Andrew N., wrote to Alexander Weir back in Gaston County, on February 7, 1853: "My father says none of you should be scared at his misfortune for it cannot be laid to our country. He has sustained his loss as a Christian ought to do, without a murmur or a groan and seems to be perfectly satisfied."[27] This was a faith that stood in the tradition of Covenanter, Seceder, Scottish Presbyterian faith. It was the faith of Scripture as these people understood Scripture. It would place the Falls family at the center of the reestablished Pisgah community, from which they would enter the social and economic life of the Arkansas River Valley.

The community was ministered to in late 1852 by the Reverend John Patrick, who had arrived a few days ahead of the second covered-wagon group. Patrick was the son of Irish parents, Charles and Isabella Patrick, "remarkable for their intelligence and piety." Though he farmed until he was nearly thirty, he wanted to become a minister. To do so, he had to go to school because the minister-farmer of a number of denominations of that day did not conform to his religious background. Though untold good was accomplished by such men, Patrick's church required an "educated ministry." As he worked his fields between the handles of a plow, the question came to his mind, "Am I pursuing my proper calling—ought not I preach the Gospel?"[28] Patrick was called to preach. The farmer-minister of many churches would have immediately gone to preaching at different stations, conducting revivals, or gathering a group of people with the hope of starting a church. Patrick, on the other hand, conformed to the demands of his church that its ministers be educated by attending both college and seminary. Patrick started to school and studied Greek. After four years, he graduated from Jefferson College at Canonsburgh, Pennsylvania, and then remained to study theology, completing his course in 1841.[29]

Because of Patrick's views on slavery, he returned to the south in 1841, where he played a role in the union of the Associate Presbytery of the

Carolinas and the Associate Reformed Synod of the South. The synod was established in 1822, when the synod of the Carolinas withdrew from the general synod. Preparation for the ministry meant, in general, that men had to travel great distances from home, usually to Pennsylvania or Ohio, to be educated for the ministry. Thus in 1836 the synod established an academy at Due West, South Carolina, designated as Erskine College in 1839. It also established a seminary at Due West in 1837. With the establishment of these institutions, the synod began a long history of educating its men for the ministry.[30]

The slavery issue, which had caused Patrick to return from the north, had been controversial among the Associate Presbyterians and the Associate Reformed Presbyterians in the south. In 1800, the Associate Presbytery had ruled against church membership for slaveholders. The Associate Reformed Church, however, made no such move, and as more Associate Reformed people bought slaves, a distance began to develop between them and the Covenanters. Many of these latter moved to the northwest to escape the issue and were joined in the second and third decades of the century by Associate Reformed people who had strong feelings about it. In 1831, the Associate Synod directed its slaveholding members to free their slaves immediately. Some ministers in the Associate Presbytery of the Carolinas migrated north because they could not enforce the ruling in their congregations, and others brought their congregations, including Pisgah and Bethany, into the Associate Reformed Synod of the South.[31]

When the Pisgah, Bethany, and other congregations joined the synod, the Associate Presbytery of the Carolinas, which they left, remained. Patrick, a probationer in the Associate church, was received as a corresponding member by the First Presbytery of the Associate Reformed Synod of the South in 1841. Shortly thereafter, efforts at union began, with Patrick serving on the joint committee on union in 1842. He was ordained by the Associate Presbytery that year. Evidence indicates that Patrick worked steadily for union, which finally occurred in 1844, when his name was added to the role of ministers in the Associate Reformed Synod of the South.[32]

For many years thereafter, Patrick was an itinerant preacher "among the vacant churches and mission fields of Virginia, east and middle Tennessee, the Carolinas, Georgia and Alabama." He toiled "amid great hardship, self-denial, and exposure. In 1849, for instance, he reported that he had preached 47 Sabbath and 13 week days, and received $51.54. Balance due him $100; of which he donated $10.46 to Domestic Missions. He made no charge for travelling expenses."[33]

Patrick went to Pope County in 1852 without appointment from the synod. He had spent the first part of the year in mission work within the bounds of the Memphis Presbytery. He was at Salem Church in west Tennessee the third and fourth Sabbaths in October, and at the suggestion of the Reverend John Wilson of that church, he went on to Pope County.[34] His arrival just before the covered-wagon caravan of 1852 was fortuitous.

Though the covered-wagon settlers had come to Arkansas seeking a new, fresh land, the continued practice of their religion was an important consideration qualifying the coming of this particular group of Scotch-Irish. The leaders would not have planned and executed the move to the west without the belief that they would have "Gospel privileges" for themselves and their children. This meant the establishment of a church in the new land in which they would build their homes. Fulfillment of this goal was nearing realization in early 1853.[35]

By then, the Reverend John Patrick had been in Pope County approximately three months. He was preparing to leave. There was consensus among the people that they should organize their church while he was there to guide them. An organizational meeting was set for Saturday, January 29, 1853, at the Potts School House on the old military road one mile west of Galley Creek. The church was organized as Pisgah, with about thirty members from thirteen families headed by John Oates IV, John Falls, James Quinn, William Oates Sr., John Oates, William Oates Jr., James Whitesides, A. N. Falls, Thomas M. Oates, John M. Ferguson, R. A. Ferguson, and Emily Ferguson.[36] It is interesting to note that Monroe Oates, who compiled the list, left out his sister Margaret Bigham but included Emily Ferguson. Both were heads of families, and each lived in her father's home. The first three on the list were reelected ruling elders.

The elders occupied positions of great responsibility as spiritual leaders of the congregation. Chosen by the people as their representatives, the ruling elders assisted in the government and discipline of the church. In church courts, their authority was equal to the minister's. At the local, or congregational level, the court was the Session, composed of the minister, who is the moderator, and the ruling elders, whose duties were "to receive members and watch over their spiritual interests."[37]

Whether receiving members by applications or testimonials, the faithful fulfillment of the duties of the Session was central to preserving the integrity of the church. Most of the founding members of the Pisgah Church were no doubt admitted by testimonials. Associate Reformed Presbyterian Standards required that a member preparing to move to a distant place apply for testimonials of his character and standing in the church, signed by the minister and one or more of the elders. Such requests were granted to those whose character was unquestioned, but under no circumstances were they given to any person "known to be corrupt in principle, or immoral in practice; or who is under pressure." Those failing to apply for their testimonials before removal could not receive them by "a subsequent application, unless the Session have reason to believe that their conversation during their absence, hath been as becometh the gospel of Christ."[38] These testimonials, if not more than a year old, entitled him "to dealing ordinances in any congregation" within the synod. Without testimonials, no person not well known to one or more of the Session could not be admitted to Communion simply on his word that he had been a member of another congregation. Without testimonials, he must submit to examination.

Members admitted by examination included those applying for baptism or for a seat at the Lord's Table for the first time, persons of other denominations (whose applications were received cautiously), those who had been absent more than a year, those without satisfactory testimonials, and those who had been formerly barred by church court from the Communion of the church and desired readmission. Applications for membership by examination were made to the Session in such a manner as to give them "sufficient time to inquire into the characters and conversation of the applications." Applicants were "examined concerning their knowledge, principles, and experience" by the minister or by the minister and one or more of the ruling elders.[39]

To the Session in that day were usually elected those who had been found to be mature Christians over a period of time, men of good judgment, compassion, and spirituality. The three original elders at Pisgah had already been elected and ordained and served as ruling elders in the Carolinas: Falls and Oates at Pisgah in North Carolina, and Quinn at Bethany in South Carolina. Falls and Oates were both in their late sixties, and Quinn was thirty-seven. The congregation knew these men, who were all related by ties of marriage, if not by blood.

A few days after the organization of Pisgah Church, Patrick left the congregation in the care of the elders and returned to his mission duties in Tennessee. The spirits of the entire colony, now consisting of approximately one hundred fifty people, had been lifted by the pioneer minister who spent thirteen weeks with them. Because he had gone to Pope County without appointment, Patrick asked for no reimbursement of expenses. The report of the Board of Domestic Missions read, "We leave it to the Synod to determine whether a man shall be paid when he acts without authority." The synod apparently thought Patrick had done good work, for it approved his expenses in the amount of forty-five dollars.[40]

With Patrick's departure, there was somewhat a feeling of void in this new outpost of old Pisgah and Bethany back in the Carolinas. Soon after he left, A. N. Falls wrote back to North Carolina: "The Rev. John Patrick left us a few days ago after spending some 12 or 13 Sabbaths with us he preached every Sabbath but one and that was one of them wet ones. I think he is well pleased with our country and if no one else comes back to preach the Gospel of glad tidings to us he will again lend us his aide he is a nobel preacher and is able to explain Gods word as deep and as easy to be understood as almost any other we maid him up $58 dollars for the time he spent with us I hope at some future day not fare distant that we will be able to raise up a church to the Lord our God the work is his we leave it to himself."[41] While some would say Falls was an optimist, the truer explanation was probably to be found in his biblical faith.

# ❊ Chapter 3 ❊

# Building a Community, 1853-1855

Organization of the Pisgah Church was a signal event for the Pope County immigrants from the Carolinas. It was a witness to a living faith in the Triune God in the hearts of the Pisgah people. They formed a church because they must, for the Christ of the church had been at the center of their ancestors' lives and at the center of theirs. As worship had nurtured them in Carolina, so would it in Pope County as their community gradually emerged. Because a search for better land gave impulse to their migration, they would use fertility and availability of land in Arkansas to encourage relatives and former neighbors in the Carolinas and Tennessee to join them. Growth of the community was paramount, for it was only through the strength of numbers that they could make legitimate requests to the synod for a regular supply of sermon. During the next two years, they would not leave community growth to chance but would work hard to recruit new emigrants to the west.

One of the strongest advocates for building the Pope County settlement was Andrew N. Falls. For years, the Arkansas people had worked especially hard to get the Alexander and Mary Oates Weir family to move to Arkansas. In the 1840s John Willson and James Bradley had urged Weir to move. Mary (Mattie) Weir's parents, William Sr. and Margaret Dickey Oates, had migrated to Arkansas in 1851. Whether Mattie's parents encouraged the Weirs to join them is unknown, but in February of 1853, Falls took up the challenge, urging Weir to aid the Pisgah settlers in building their colony: "I donte think it a miss to ask you to lend us thine aide under the presant circumstances. You have a large familey and I think you can do much better buy them hear than theire. They work is commenced and now is the time to put forth your hand and lend us thine aide." Falls continued, "I no the land is much better and a great deal cheaper. We have other advantages that you have not. Our country is fresh and range good; yours is old and range done. I have not fed a cow this Winter and they are fat in the cain." There were other advantages. In Arkansas there was the river instead of railroads. "We all send to New Orleans for groceryes: Coffee 9¢ Shugar 100 lbs for 5 dollars. Molases 25¢ pr. Gal. Salt 1.80 pr Sack. Rice 4 and 5¢ pr pound. How much better can you do in your old settled country Rail Roade and all?" He urged Weir to make a decision: "If you have any notion of coming you would do well to not put it of too longe. Our valley is fast filling up with new comers. We have had a good many this Fall and Winter. If you come solicit as many as will. I have entered 527 Acres and I gave 425 dollars for 120 acres the last purchase I maide." Falls clearly related the economic advantages to church building: "When we settled hear we seen that theire was opening for a large church if you will onely except the offer."[1]

Though Falls failed to persuade Weir to emigrate, members of the Bethany community in York District, South Carolina, were contemplating a move in the spring of 1853: William (1791–1870) and Betsy Neely McElwee (1797–1863). McElwee had lived in the South Carolina upper country all of his life. His family, who were of Irish stock, established themselves in York County in 1765, where John and William McElwee III were among the founders and elders of the Bethany Associate Reformed Presbyterian Church.[2] By fall of 1853, William and his family were ready to move.

The McElwee migration was another of the "family moves" that characterized the movements to Pope County. Just as John Oates IV and William Oates Sr. had led the migration of 1851, and John Falls that of 1852, so William McElwee led the migration of 1853. It is uncertain who constituted the party, but they probably included William and Betsy Neely McElwee and their children who were still at home—Nancy, Samuel, Elizabeth, and James; their son John R., his wife, Isabella McMahon McElwee, and their family; their son James, his wife, Jane McElwee McElwee, and their family; their daughter Eliza (1812–1885), her husband, John F. Oates V (1813–1859), and their family; and their daughter Melissa (1829–1900), her husband, Thomas Oates (1821–1904), and their family. William McElwee Jr. remained behind as a student at Due West, South Carolina. He, Monroe Oates, son of John Oates IV, and Erskine College classmate William Hood watched the McElwee caravan as it moved out, headed to the west. According to Nancy D. McElwee, who was an adult when she made the journey, there were seventy people in the wagon train, apparently including the slaves these families took with them. Among the latter were Rosa, Abigail, and Abigail's son Frank, held in trust for Isabella McElwee by John F. Oates.[3]

According to Hood, it was late in the fall when the caravan of wagons and cattle started on the long, tiresome journey: "When they started, they dropped down into South Carolina in order to flank the North Carolina mountains, and then swung back to the original line, and passed out of Georgia into Tennessee at Chattanooga, thence to Memphis, and on westward following very nearly the same line, and finally settled very nearly on the same latitude they had lived in North Carolina, shaded here and there in the new home by mountain spurs very much apparently as they had been in the old home. We talked very much of them and watched their progress together while they were out by means of maps." They could chart the progress, Hood said, because Monroe Oates and his cousin William McElwee received letters from their families while they were en route.[4]

The party had arrived in Pope County by early December, for on the twelfth, John F. Oates V bought eighty acres of land.[5] Others followed suit and soon settled in. Thomas M. Oates wrote to Alexander Weir and family in North Carolina: "Those that came in last Fall has all got homes. Franklin Oates bought 240 acres of land and give thirteen hundred dollars for it. It was very well improved and old Mr. Mcellwee bought 120 acres for $1200 and paid it nearly all in gold but is well pleas at the place."[6]

Meanwhile, in the fall, Tennessean Alexander K. Dickey had appeared at Pisgah. Before he had moved to Wayne County, Tennessee, in 1833, he had lived in the Pisgah community in North Carolina and was thoroughly anchored in the web of family relationships at Pisgah in Pope County. His nephew, William Oates Jr., had been in the advance party of 1850, and his sister Margaret Dickey Oates had come with her husband and several members of the family to Arkansas in 1851. The purpose of Dickey's visit was to look over land. Before he left Arkansas for his home in Tennessee, he bought eighty acres.[7] Thus with prospects of another migration, 1854 promised to be a year of high hopes for the Pisgah settlers in the Arkansas River Valley.

One of their most important undertakings was what Andrew Nael Falls had called "raising up a church to the Lord our God." A site for a church building was first selected in a beautiful grove near the eastern border of what was then known as Shue Prairie. The New Madrid earthquake of 1811 devastated the delta region in northeastern Arkansas. In later years the United States government offered land grants to those whose homesteads had been in what was known as the "sunken lands." Among those who received land were the Shues, who settled near what is now Pottsville. Some building materials were placed on the ground at Shue Prairie, but the site was reconsidered and another rather more centrally located to the Associate Reformed Presbyterian settlers was chosen, about four miles southeast of present-day Russellville and two southeast of Pottsville. The title to this latter four-acre site was executed and delivered by D. Cicero and Lucretia Harkey for thirty-five dollars.[8]

Though the Scots-Irish had a strong bent toward simplicity in their services, they chose a location that would have graced an Old World cathedral when they selected a site for their church building. The place was on a high hill that gradually sloped on the north side into a deep valley. Beyond the valley were hills in an ascending order. Crow Mountain formed a circular curtain behind the hills, and above Crow Mountain the sky framed all. Looking another way in the distance could be seen the biblically named Mount Nebo draped in changing colors of blue. The site reflected a phrase from the Psalms: "beautiful for situation." Today, standing at the marker of old Pisgah Church, one can still take in this magnificent sweep of the landscape. In addition to its beauty, the site had another advantage: the churchyard that was to be used as a "burying ground" was well drained.

By March 1854, construction had begun. The settlers devised a plan whereby each family was supposed to deliver on the ground their part of the lumber for the frame church. Thomas Oates wrote to a cousin in the Carolinas, "We have started to bild a church. we have got out part of the timber. It is to be thirty by forty feet with a 14 ft story. We all agree very well. We want to have it ready for to preach in by the time the Rev. J. K. Boyce gets here. He says that he will be here about July if permitted by divine providence."[9]

Back in North Carolina, Alexander Weir was again asking questions about Arkansas, as he had done for more than a decade. This time, Thomas Oates took up where John Willson, the Bradleys, and most recently, Andrew Nael Falls had left off. Weir had asked Oates to write, as he said, "and tell you wheather I thot you could do any better here than you can on them Sandy ridges." First, regarding productivity of the land and the ability to market goods, Oates claimed Weir would be able to double his production in Pope County with the same amount of work. Oates sent word to his Cousin William Weir that he thought "he had better leave them hill sides for some one else to work and come to Arkansas ware the land is better." The elder Weir was also apparently contemplating Fulton County, Arkansas, which had a growing Associate Reformed Presbyterian community, as a possible site for resettlement. Oates met the argument head-on that Fulton County was a better place than Pope: "their may be very good land their, but uncle James Montgomery says that is not a good plase for a settlement. They have fine corn and wheat country but not so good for cotton and they are some forty or fifty miles from market."

Second, Pope County was conducive to good health, which, Oates declared, is "very uncertain any whare." He had been in Pope County two seasons; "the first was very sickley and the last was very healthy. As for my part I have had better health than I had in Carolina." Of Fulton County, he wrote, "As for health I think it is no better than it is here." Thus on the score of productivity of Arkansas land and healthfulness, he concluded: "Therefore I think you can do agrate deal better here than their that is if you can be satisfied."

Oates also knew that their Scots heritage of Christian faith was important to the Weirs. He was like the Baptist preacher who was once asked if he preached on baptism in every sermon. His answer was, "No, I don't preach on baptism every Sunday, but I do sprinkle it in, in every sermon." Oates sprinkled references to their common faith throughout the letter. They were building a church structure, and they had hopes that an educated minister would settle among them. "We understand that our good friend the Rev. John Patrick is going to get married and we hope he will come to Arkansas and settle." Then Oates played a trump card: "Our church is increasing as uncle Alexander Dickey is going to move here and is perhaps on the road now. He has bought land here and has sold his land in Tennessee." Dickey was the maternal uncle of Alexander Weir's wife.

Oates urged Weir to make a decision and not put it off. "Their is considerable excitement here about the railroad," he wrote. An engineer was surveying a route and had reached a point only twelve miles from Pisgah. If the route ran the way the engineer said it would, the tracks would be within one mile of Oates's home. The prospects of a railroad had caused "land to rise." He added, "It is the generally opinion of the friends here that those that intend to leave North Carolina and move to Pope County had better come soon or it may be to their disadvantage."[10] Oates asked Weir who from the old community he thought would come in the fall of 1854, if any.

Though Oates failed to entice the Weirs to emigrate, Alexander Dickey made the trek from Tennessee, as Oates had predicted. Dickey had gone to Arkansas in 1853, bought a farm, and returned home in early 1854. The relatives in Pope County, especially his sister Margaret, wife of William Oates Sr., no doubt began to look forward to the Dickeys' arrival. The web of family connections would also cause the Gregory Sinclair family to come to the county. Dickey (1796–1866), a native of Lincoln County, North Carolina, and his wife, Jannice (Jenny) Sinclair Dickey (1799–1876), a native of Ireland, had moved to Tennessee in 1833, settling first in Wayne County and then Hardin County, where they remained until they removed to Pope County, taking with them their unmarried children, while their married children remained at Fayetteville and Savannah, Tennessee.[11]

Another family enriched the Pisgah community in 1854: Alexander (1804–1882) and Mary Oates Bell (1814–1881), who brought their entire family with them to Pope County. Mary had many relatives in the community already, her brother William Oates Jr., one of the advance scouting party, being among the first to arrive. The Bell caravan followed the route taken by earlier migrants from Gaston County: by way of Greenville, South Carolina, to Decatur and Rome, Georgia, along the Tennessee-Alabama line to Memphis, with a stop in Wayne County, Tennessee to visit relatives. From Memphis they traveled by water to Prairie County, Arkansas, where they began the last leg of their journey by wagon.[12]

Hugh Taylor was also in the Pisgah community by late 1854 when he bought land. When the Taylor family migrated from Tennessee and whether they came alone or with others is uncertain. However, by the spring of 1856 he had found his place in the community and the church, when he was chosen a ruling elder.[13] Also, Mrs. E. Kirkpatrick and D. S. Kirkpatrick were in the community by 1854, for they appear on the tax rolls.[14]

Early in 1855, a Wayne County, Tennessee, family, the Gregory Sinclairs, were on the threshold of a move to Pope County. The Sinclairs by all accounts were "reasonably prosperous" in Tennessee, but according to their grandson, their move was the result of a strong brother-sister relationship: "His sister Jennie Dickey and family had previously moved to Pope County, Arkansas. Since Gregory and Jennie had been almost inseparable, he decided to move to Arkansas."[15]

Samuel and Rebecca Barrett Sinclair, who had identified themselves with the Seceders, married in Scotland and emigrated to Cookstown, County Tyrone, Ireland, where they were members of the Associate Church of Sandholes, the same congregation to which some ancestors of the Oates family had belonged. There, they leased eight acres from Lady Hamilton, farmed, and raised their family. The children of Samuel and Rebecca Barrett Sinclair were Samuel, John, Margaret, William, Gregory (1796–1876), and Jennie. The elder Sinclair was a veterinary surgeon and a thatcher, while his son John was a farmer and the other sons weavers of linen. Samuel was a lover of music and sang as he worked at the loom all day. Family tradition has it that Jennie sang Samuel's compositions, one of which had these lines:

> She lifted her petticoat 'way above her knee
> and danced for gingerbread to put in her tea.[16]

Their life was difficult in Ireland. John cultivated the eight acres of potatoes and flax and prepared the flax for spinning, with Margaret and Jennie assisting with the latter. Samuel, William, and Gregory worked at their two looms eighteen hours a day. Thus they resolved to emigrate to America. After Rebecca and young Samuel died, they made their move. On September 19, 1817, William and Gregory Sinclair sailed from Belfast on the English ship *Elizabeth* and arrived at Charleston, South Carolina, on November 1. A Mr. Hamilton, an old friend of their father, kept them four days and then they went on to Crowder's Creek west of Gastonia, North Carolina, to the home of their cousin John Blackwood.[17]

Two years later, they owned a farm and had saved enough to help bring the rest of the family to America. In 1819, Samuel and his children John, Margaret, and Jennie, arrived in Baltimore. John walked to Gastonia, got a one-horse wagon, and returned to Baltimore for the family. According to Neill H. Bell, this migration attested to the Sinclair ruggedness: "when William and Gregory came to America they walked the eighteen miles from their home to Belfast; also, that when they reached Charleston they walked the full distance from Charleston to the Blackwood home near Kings Mountain, a distance which exceeds two hundred miles. This same characteristic is shown, likewise, by the second group of the family when it came to America to join the others. These, being forced to disembark at Baltimore, were yet more than three hundred miles from the recently acquired home in North Carolina. In this instance, John walked the entire distance while the parent and daughters walked in turns and, with family belongings, occupied the small one-horse wagon."[18]

In 1833, the family moved once more, this time to Wayne County, Tennessee, in search of more and better land. Members of the Associate Church in Ireland, they had been members of the Pisgah Church in Lincoln County, North Carolina, and remained faithful to their church practices in Tennessee. Gregory married Margaret Blackwood (1807–1888), daughter of John Blackwood, and lived on Pinhook farm on Weatherford Creek at the time they decided to move to Pope County to join Jennie and her husband, Alexander Dickey, who had moved the year before.[19]

The family of Margaret Blackwood Sinclair also came from County Tyrone, Ireland, but much earlier. Margaret's grandfather had migrated to North Carolina, near Kings Mountain in 1760, where he owned a store, a blacksmith shop, and a gristmill, and was instrumental in supplying arms and supplies for the battle of Kings Mountain. Margaret's father, John, had five brothers and one sister. He married Jeanette Reed Bradshaw, who bore him three sons and five daughters. Among the latter, besides Margaret, was Anna, who with her husband, William MacIntosh, and family moved to Arkansas with the Sinclairs. According to Neill Bell, the MacIntoshes came as "an appeasement" to Margaret Blackwood Sinclair, "since she was breaking with her family in the move to Arkansas."[20]

As the Sinclair and MacIntosh families prepared to move, Gregory Sinclair sold his farm, household goods, and other property. Among the latter was Nancy, a slave, who had been a nurse to his young daughter Mary Ann (Molly). "It was hard indeed," Molly would later write, "for me to give up Nancy as she ranked next to my mother with me."[21]

The covered wagons carrying the Sinclairs and MacIntoshes left Wayne County on January 16, 1855. According to Mary Ann Sinclair Falls, there were seventeen in the group. The party traveled by way of Florence, Alabama, where they took a boat down the Tennessee River to the Ohio, down that stream to the Mississippi, down that to Napoleon, at the mouth of the Arkansas, that part of the trip taking about two weeks. The party was delayed there by low water until March 19. Their travel up the Arkansas was slow, the captain of the boat being cautious. They finally reached Lewisburg and could go no further. There Sinclair left the group with William MacIntosh and went ahead to Alexander Dickey's home near Pisgah.[22] He wrote that night, "I have on my person six hundred and twenty-four dollars in gold, forty dollars in paper and twenty-four dollars in silver." The date was April 5, 1855.[23]

Alexander Dickey and Sinclair returned to Lewisburg for the family. Before they left there, the Sinclairs suffered a painful loss of a beloved slave. Mary Ann Sinclair Falls wrote, "Just before we were ready to leave Lewisburg, our old 'black mother Rhine' died. This was another heart-breaking scene with us. After we had buried her near that place, we departed in the wagons." The Sinclairs and MacIntoshes, with Alexander and James Dickey's help, arrived at Pisgah. They were received with open arms by the Pisgah people, and none more so than Alex and Jennie Sinclair Dickey. Gregory Sinclair immediately bought land and reestablished himself.[24]

Sinclair built an impressive home, "two and a half stories high, with a 'dog trot' through the middle downstairs, and the kitchen in a section jutting off one end of the back." It "was constructed in part by slaves, its beams and the other heavy parts of the frame hewn from oak timber. Hand dressed pine boards went into the siding and floors. Cypress shingles covered the roof—and weren't replaced for sixty years." Chimneys in the house were made of brick and the kitchen chimney of stone. In later years, the family presumed that the "hardware, window glass, and such items" came from New Orleans.[25]

Gregory Sinclair's life journey had carried him far. In thirty-eight years he made three major moves, from Ireland to North Carolina, to Tennessee, and to Pope County, Arkansas. He was rugged, determined, thrifty, industrious, and deeply religious. His hobbies were Irish songs and "orthography." His daughter Mary Ann remembered his frequently entertaining with his "original songs, spelling and defining words."[26]

South Carolina furnished more immigrants to Pisgah colony that year. Monroe Oates writes, "Mr. John Harbison came from Sharon, York County, South Carolina in company with Mr. J. M. Henry in 1855." James

Henry was married to John and Elizabeth Harbison's daughter Mary J. In addition to Mary J., three other of Harbison's children came with the party. Oates also indicated that James G. and Martha Hays and their family migrated from Tennessee that year and joined the Pisgah settlement.[27]

The continued immigration during 1854 and 1855 of families with like religious beliefs resulted in a corresponding growth in the Pisgah Church. In the summer of 1853, the Reverend John K. Boyce spent a few Sabbaths with them.[28] Boyce returned again in the summer of 1854, at which time the Session, consisting of Boyce and the three original Pisgah elders, concluded that the number of elders needed to be increased. They nominated Alexander Dickey, recently arrived from Tennessee, John Franklin Oates V from South Carolina, and Andrew Nael Falls, whose names were placed before a meeting of the people.[29] Falls was elected and Dickey and Oats reelected because they had been elected ruling elders in their churches before their migration to the west. Having been ordained already, Dickey and Oates would need only to be installed, while Falls would be ordained and then installed.

At the ordination ceremony, Boyce propounded to Falls the questions that constituted the ordination vows according to the standards of the church. He began: "Do you believe the holy scriptures of the Old and New Testaments to be the word of the living God; the perfect and only rule of faith and practice, to which nothing is to be added, and from which nothing is to be taken, at any time, or upon any pretext, whether of new revelations of the Spirit or traditions of men?" Next, "Do you receive the doctrine of this church, contained in her Confession and Catechisms, as founded on the word of God, and as the expression of your own faith? and do you resolve to adhere thereto, in opposition to all Deistical, Popish, Arian, Socinian, Arminian, Neonomian, and Sectarian errors, and all other opinions which are contrary to sound doctrine and the power of godliness?" The next two questions affirmed his adherence to church government and directories for worship and his submission to the decisions of the church courts. The next two examined his motives for taking the office of ruling elder. And the next two affirmed his resolve in discipline of the family and the church. Finally, "Do you make these promises as in the presence of Him, who searcheth the hearts, and trieth the reins of the children of men; and as you would desire to give in your account with joy at the great day of the Redeemer's appearance, when He shall come, and all his saints with him?"

Besides helping to strengthen church governance during his brief visit at Pisgah, Boyce also dispensed the Lord's Supper. In perhaps no other practice of religion is the cohesion of the church and church community reflected more than in the observance of this sacrament. The "end of Christian communion," according to the standards of the Associate Reform Presbyterian Church, is *edification,* "and the means by which Christ edifies, or builds up, His people and His church are *the sound principles of His Gospel, His ordinances in their purity and integrity,* and *faithful discipline.* Whatever corrupts and impairs these means mars edification. Communion, therefore, should not be extended when extending it would give countenance to dangerous error, corrupt worship, or sin. To admit to the Lord's table individuals holding to error, or corrupt worship, or notoriously belonging to societies which so hold, would have this effect." The church guarded against this by holding to "explicit terms of communion," which "should be faithfully maintained; and the church cannot consistently admit to membership those who are hostile to her principles, nor to occasional communion at the Lord's table those who cannot be received into regular membership."[30]

Strict adherence to "explicit terms of communion" and requirements concerning psalmody set the Associate Reformed Presbyterians apart from other Presbyterians. It was on the same basis that the church's historians in the late nineteenth century could claim that in doctrine and practice, it had "retained more of the Scotch type of Presbyterianism, as it existed prior to the reign of Charles II., than any other branch of the Presbyterian Church in America."[31]

The "explicit terms of communion" are expressed in the Principles of Church Fellowship as recorded in the church standards. It was the duty of the Session to carefully attend to the principles, as follows: admission to baptism and the Lord's Supper is the solemn recognition of visible membership in the church. Both sacraments are seals of the covenant of grace and cannot be disjoined. All baptized persons "are bound by the baptismal vow, to show forth the Lord's death, when arrived at the years of discretion; and are the lawful subjects of church government." Visible membership "may be forfeited by open renunciation of Christ's truth, . . . by evident want of acquaintance with its power, . . . or by unholy conduct." Thus, "no person, though baptized, may be admitted to a seat at the table of the Lord, or to baptism for his children, unless his profession and practice afford sufficient reason, in the judgment of charity, that he is a member of the church invisible."[32]

The Lord's Supper, in this belief, reflects not only one's commitment to duty regarding his own spiritual well-being and regarding his fellow members of the visible church but also his commitment to duty regarding his children. An unbaptized person can not be admitted to the table of the Lord or to baptism for his children. Those who dedicate their children in baptism are, on admission to that privilege, "strictly enjoined to act consistently in their profession, by celebrating, in the sacrament of the supper, the dying love of the Lord Jesus." Those who offer their children in baptism but abstain from the sacrament of the supper and persist in neglecting that ordinance are, "after solemn and frequent admonitions" by church officers, "debarred from every sacramental service." But in cases in which persons present their children in baptism, but are "deterred by darkness of mind, distressing fears, or strong temptations, from approaching the table of the Lord," it is the duty of the officers of the church, particularly the minister, "to use every gentle and persuasive method for removing their difficulties." Those who have been admitted to the Lord's table and afterward neglect that ordinance are, after due but ineffectual admonition, "judicially excluded from the privileges of the church."

In thinking about Sacrament time at Pisgah, it is important to know the atmosphere of the occasion. Whatever sparks faith generated during the year, the sparks were intensified at the Communion Services. Even the youth caught the idea that mystery was present. The feeling of mystery about what Christ had done on the Cross was there, but it was a mystery that was not without light. Somehow they sensed Christ had done this for them—that their grudges could be forgiven, that they could be reconciled to a neighbor, that husbands and wives could be more considerate of one another—and that sinful though they were, they could be forgiven and lead a new life.

The Season of Sacrament did not gloss over sin—it exposed it and its consequences. But this was not the last word. The Gospel was the Good News, the death of Christ for their sin. The Sacrament exposed guilt, but the Cross of Christ gave the way of escape—the Cross revealed the forgiveness for those, who in true penitence, turned to Christ in faith for His salvation.

There were few Pisgah people who had a pious vocabulary, but by and large they were people who took the Bible as the Word of God to them. Sometimes they expressed their feelings bluntly, and some could not verbalize what was inside them, sometimes crying to be said at Sacrament time. The mystery of God in Christ was there, and in the preaching of the Word, the prayers, the singing of the Psalms, the Cup and Bread, given and received, their needs were being exposed and met by the Grace of God if they were receptive to the Word of God that was coming to them.

The preparatory services for the observance of the Lord's Supper and the celebration of the Sacrament on the Sabbath constituted a special occasion at Pisgah. The members of the church organized their life around this important event. Preparatory services were held at the church during the week before the Sabbath. Only field work that had to be done was done. "If the ox was in the ditch, he had to be pulled out," but otherwise the routines of everyday life were somewhat relaxed. For the women, their work continued. The family had to be fed, clothes made ready for wearing to church. The routine of cooking and baking was even accelerated in some homes for there might be as many as ten or more guests at the Sabbath table.

On the Sabbath, families gathered at the church amidst an expectant air. A meeting of the Session determined who would serve the bread and the cup. According to the doctrines of the church, "Before coming to the Lord's table, communicants should *examine* themselves of their knowledge to discern the Lord's body, of their faith to feed upon Him, and of their repentance, love, and new obedience, lest, coming unworthily, they should dishonor Christ and bring guilt and divine displeasure on their souls." The minister invited those who were repentant and faithful to come forward to the table on which were the elements of the Lord's Supper. Holding up a piece of bread, he said, "Take, eat; this is my body which is broken for you; do this in remembrance of me," and handed the bread plates to the elders who proceeded to serve the congregation. He took the cup and using Christ's words, said, "After the same manner also he took the cup, when he had supped, saying, 'This is the New Testament in my blood; this do ye as oft as ye drink it, in remembrance of me.' For as often as ye eat this bread and drink this cup, ye do show the Lord's death till He come." Then he handed the cup to the elders to serve the people. After the congregation was served, the minister served the elders and then was himself served.

In addition to the services, the visits the Reverend Boyce made to the homes of the congregation in 1853 and 1854 must have made a profound impression upon Pisgah, for thirty years later, Monroe Oates wrote: "His visits were very satisfactory to the church especially as he was very pointed in reminding the heads of families of their duties and conversed with the young concerning their spiritual interests."[33]

When Andrew Nael Falls wrote to Alexander Weir that he hoped his community would soon "be able to raise up a church to the Lord our God," he was referring to "raising" up a place of worship, a church building. Pisgah had its church in 1854. It also elected three strong new elders, doubling the number of the members in the Session. The church was growing by the addition of new members. The first Communion Service had been held in the new building. But they had no minister, and their need for one was growing.

The prospects of their obtaining one were enhanced by a growing Associate Reformed Presbyterian presence in Arkansas. Several families, principally from Tennessee and Georgia, had settled in Fulton County and would eventually establish Prosperity Church. Another growing community was at Monticello in Drew County. News came to Pisgah in March 1855 that a church had been organized there in February. The history of the Monticello Church was similar to Pisgah's. In 1853–54 some Associate Reformed Presbyterian families had moved from Tipton County, Tennessee, to Drew County. The Reverend J. K. Boyce visited these families, just as he had Pisgah, during his missionary tour in the summer of 1854. The following winter, the Reverend John Wilson of the Salem Church in Tipton County spent several weeks in the community and organized the church, and construction of a church building began. In the fall of 1854, the Associate Reformed Synod of the South responded to the growing needs of the Arkansas communities by placing the three mission stations under the care of the Memphis Presbytery. The synod assigned the Reverend A. S. Montgomery to spend six months in Arkansas in 1855, dividing his time among the communities. However, he failed to meet his appointment because of illness in the family.[34]

That summer, however, the Pisgah community was animated by the arrival of the Reverend John Patrick, who had not been in Pisgah since February of 1853, when he organized the church. The fact that the fifty-year-old bachelor had taken a wife only increased the interest in his visit.

In the back of the minds of the Pisgah people was the thought that Providence might be leading Patrick to a residence at Pisgah to be their minister. For years he had gone over the southern states preaching the Gospel; he was not so young as he once was, and maybe he was being called to a more settled existence.

Soon after Patrick's visit, the Session of Pisgah Church started correspondence with representatives of the synod about securing Patrick's services half-time. They were rewarded, for in November, Patrick and his wife, Mary E., came to Pisgah. The people at Pisgah did not supply their minister with a manse, and after weeks of search, Patrick found 140 acres in the Cove, where he would build a house.[35] With the arrival of a minister who could provide a supply of sermons on a regular basis, the people of the Pisgah community took a major step forward in the organization of their community.

# ❋ Chapter 4 ❋

# Economic Prosperity

John Falls, one of the founding elders at Pisgah, died on July 4, 1855, and was buried in the Pisgah Cemetery. In his will, Falls apportioned his earthly goods, lands, and chattels among his heirs. He was a man of substance, despite having uprooted his household, moving several hundred miles to the west, and starting over in a new land. His quick economic recovery was typical of the Pisgah settlers. Unlike many who arrived poverty stricken in the west, these were people of means who brought their resources with them, and their arrival in Pope County quickly revolutionized the economy of the region.

Falls and other Pisgah settlers timed their migrations to advantage. Nearly all occurred in the fall. Occasionally, delays resulted in a party's being caught in the rainy weeks of late winter, but for the most part, they traveled in the dry season of fall, arriving in Pope County in time to buy land and settle in before spring planting time. Arriving with the means to reestablish themselves quickly, they did not miss a planting season. The consensus was that their land in Pope County was much more fertile than that they had left in the Carolinas. A good first crop might have more than compensated for many of the losses sustained in a move of the magnitude that they had undertaken.

The arrival of the Pisgah covered-wagon settlers, in fact, transformed land ownership patterns in the county. It was common before 1850 for Pope County settlers simply to take up and improve land, which they claimed by right of occupancy. In 1851, one study shows, only somewhat over 24 percent of residents who paid poll taxes also paid taxes on land. By 1860, however, the figures dramatically changed. Taxed acreage increased by 138 percent, and the number of landless heads of household decreased from about 76 to about 66 percent.[1] The Pisgah settlers contributed greatly to this progress, for nearly all bought land upon their arrival or within a short time thereafter. In his letter to Alexander Weir in early 1853, Andrew Nael Falls had accurately predicted a time soon to come when the security of ownership would rest in title rather than squatter's rights.[2] Such expressions of concern to new arrivals who had ready means to buy may explain in part the immediacy of many land purchases. Too, they arrived with the idea of putting down permanent roots, while economic and social forces tempted some of their fellow countians to move on.

The Pisgah settlers were a part of great migrations to the American West that occurred in the 1850s. The year the advance party had made their scouting expedition, the great Gold Rush to California had got under way. The Arkansas River Valley provided the main travel route through Arkansas to Van Buren and Fort Smith, which became a major staging area for wagon trains headed to California. Some Pope Countians gave in to the lure of California, which was much in the news in Pope County as elsewhere. In 1851, Kirkbride Potts had driven a herd of cattle to California and sold them in the gold fields, returning in early 1852. J. R. Homer Scott of Dover, member of another prominent local family, had decided by 1851 that he, too, would try his fortune and health in California. The following spring, he sent his brother the names of a number of relatives and acquaintances who had already gone, and later that year, Scott himself headed west with a large herd of cattle to sell in the gold fields, returned, and undertook another drive in 1853, arriving in California in September with 130 head. Other Pope County citizens organized cattle drives to California. In 1855, Dr. McFadden was reported to have made two drives, and in 1856, Potts and W. H. Rankin organized drives as did Rankin, Thomas J. Linton, and others in 1857.[3]

Whether they went with intentions to stay or return, Pope Countians departed for California for its promise of economic opportunity. Some succeeded. Others found life difficult there and saw their hopes fade. George A. Scott, for instance, lost all he had in a storekeeping venture in the gold fields. By May 1853 he was determined to return home and was working hard to save in order to make the return trip. "But it matters not with me be it hard or easy," he wrote his brother Henry, "so I make it honestly and enough to justify my return to my own Native Land, Arkansas."[4] Like his brother, J. R. Homer Scott found California expensive, and though he did not make the profit he had hoped on his cattle drive of 1853, it was sufficient to justify his effort, "considering," he said,

"I am from Arkansas where every man is a bankrupt and those who are not, fast merging toward it." He dreaded the thought of spending his remaining days in Pope County and rearing his children there: "At any place in any state or clime but Arkansas, I could expect to rear them as I would desire, but this State, especially where I live, is peculiarly cursed for ignorance, poverty, want of good society, etc. and I have been so long chained to the spot and poverty, that I could not extricate myself."[5] Upon his return to Pope County in 1854, he was "perfectly lost"; "everything so dull here, no business, no life, nothing prepossessing out side my family." He wanted to make another trek across the plains, but family and other matters prevented it. He had thought of building a steam gristmill, but there was too little money in the country to make it pay.[6]

Scott was animated by reports in 1855 that gold had been discovered in the Wichita Mountains in the western Choctaw Nation. "Should these discoveries prove true and I think they will," he wrote, "the 'Sleep' of Arkansas is over and she will awake to the reality that she was slumbering *only* and that a brighter day awaits her and her destiny be linked with the brightest." Two years later, Scott was still writing about how dull life was in Pope County because his business in Dover was poor.[7]

The extent of the migrations from Pope County may never be known but it was apparently significant if the Scott family correspondence offers a fair estimate. The migration of young men had continued through the decade so that by 1857 the supply of eligible bachelors had so dwindled that some "forty or more girls that want to marry" in the Dover community were reported in jeopardy of becoming old maids.[8]

California did not hold any great appeal for the covered-wagon settlers at Pisgah. From the earliest settlers in the 1840s to A. N. Falls and other members of the first and second great migrations, their appeals to others to join them had touted good land. In Pope County, they found the land they sought and liked the land they found. They had mostly gone long distances in search of the land they now possessed. They faced the challenges that went with clearing land and building houses and farmsteads, but their spirits were lifted by the opportunities before them. Thus while the California fever raged about them and many people left the county to follow their dreams, the Pisgah settlers remained and built theirs. They stayed, encouraged others to join them, and built a stable community centered in their church.

The rapidity with which they reestablished themselves in Pope County suggests that much of the land they bought was cleared or otherwise improved. Land prices varied according to fertility and the extent of improvements on the tract. Most of the Pisgah settlers who came between 1850 and the end of 1855 paid prices equal to, or above, the going price for improved land in 1858, five to ten dollars an acre or higher. In 1851, for example, A. N. Falls paid $5.43 an acre for one tract. In 1853, he paid $11.25, while Alexander Dickey and John F. Oates V paid $5. In 1854, John Oates IV and Thomas Oates paid $5, William McElwee paid $10, Alex Dickey $16.25, and James Quinn $12.50. In 1855, Gregory Sinclair paid $8.13, William B. Dickey $6.67, and John F. Oates V $15. A recent study of Pope County land singles out purchases by Falls, Franklin Oates, and McElwee at $3.35, $5.41, and $10 an acre, respectively. "Although most settlers acquired homesteads at prices well below this trio," the author writes, "some regarded even substantially lower prices as prohibitive."[9] The higher prices paid by the Pisgah settlers testify to their substance, their means to buy higher quality land, and their intent to provide for their families.

Geography determined where they established their new homes. The Arkansas River, which the early Carolina settlers had touted as their substitute for railroads, presented obstacles. The river bottoms offered the best soil for growing cotton, but held the twin risks of ill health and crop loss by flooding. The bottoms were the breeding ground of "the fever," malaria. Settlers in the region had learned that lesson early and generally found the bottoms unfit for habitation, and crops planted there were at risk of being flooded, as three major floods in the 1830s and early 1840s had shown.[10] Pisgah settlers, arriving the next decade, had the benefit of the earlier settlers' experience. Though some bought parcels of the alluvial bottom land, for the most part they settled on the rolling hills of the land rising from the river toward Crow Mountain, with their members concentrated in Illinois and Galley Rock townships.

Geography also determined the kinds of farmers they would be in Arkansas. The hilly countryside was not conducive to large-scale agriculture. Thus the Pisgah holdings tended to be modest and better suited to crops other than cotton. As farmers, the Pisgah settlers engaged in diversified subsistence farming with cotton raised in small quantities on the side as a potential cash crop.[11] In short, they were not planters but self-sufficient, yeoman farmers who in many ways fit Jefferson's agrarian model of the ideal American, but some of them owned slaves. So did Jefferson.

The major crops grown at Pisgah during the 1850s, in descending order, were corn, wheat, and oats. There was, as well, an occasional small acreage of rye. Wheat provided feed for livestock as well as breadstuffs for the household. Oat production declined dramatically in Pope County during the 1850s. One study argues that the decreased production of oats, high-energy-value food for draft animals, indicates that local farmers did not raise draft animals for the market. The author writes, "Analysis of the 1860 county agricultural census reveals that except for Illinois township all the major oat producing townships within the county grew oats at levels commensurate with the number of farms within the township. Only Illinois produced 8 percent more oats than its percentage of farms would predict, possibly because drayage activities at the Norristown landing required that draft animals receive year long supplemental feed." The explanation of these statistics may rest, rather, in the presence of the large number of Pisgah settlers in the township, about 75 percent of whom were growing oats in 1860. Also, this same study ties oat culture to "a commitment to agricultural excellence,"[12] which reflects favorably on the Pisgah farmers, who apparently maintained a higher-than-average production of the grain.

Corn was by far the major crop for Pisgah farmers as it was for other farmers in the county. Corn production in Pope County rose during the decade to a per-capita average one-half bushel greater than the state average. This rise can be attributed, in part perhaps, to the continued arrival of Pisgah settlers who nearly to a farmer raised corn, some in huge quantities.[13]

Their extensive production of corn can be explained by the livestock herds maintained by Pisgah farmers, particularly the large herds of hogs. Swine production increased in Pope County during the 1850s, and in 1860 stood above the state average production of 2.6 swine per capita at 3.3. In contrast to the large swine herds they maintained, the Pisgah farmers kept small herds of cattle, horses, and mules and small flocks of sheep. Herds of cattle, horses, and mules at Pisgah seem to reflect the trends of the 1850s. By 1860, few of the Pisgah farmers maintained work oxen, a large percentage of the cattle herds consisting of milk cows. These facts reflect the county trends of declining use of horses and oxen as draft animals and the rising use of mules, as do the small numbers of horses reported, suggesting their use primarily as transportation. Sheep flocks and wool production for the making of cloth varied among Pisgah settlers. Some raised no sheep, but the Oates, Falls, Bell, Bigham, Wells, and Ferguson families, for example, maintained flocks commonly numbering from ten to fifteen.[14]

Cotton was the major cash crop for some Pisgah farmers. During the 1850s, cotton production increased in Pope County, though the number of households engaging in cotton production remained stable. While cotton production increased in both slaveless and slave households, by far the greater increase was among the latter.[15]

Once more, Pisgah farmers do not conform to average statistics for the county. The 33 identified Pisgah slaveholders owned 150 slaves, or 17 percent of the slaves in Pope County and 30 percent of those in Illinois and Galley Rock townships. Silas R. Parker, who owned 24, the largest number, raised no cotton at all in 1860 but had his slaves engaged in raising tobacco and other crops. The same was true of Margaret M. Bigham, who owned 7 slaves. Eliza E. Oates, however, who owned 13 slaves, the second largest number, reported 25 bales of cotton. A. N. Falls, who had only 3 slaves, reported 7 bales. Franklin R. Bell, who owned no slaves, reported 4 bales, while John R. McElwee, who owned 7, reported no cotton at all.[16]

Of course, the production of any crops, whether for local consumption or the market, depended on a number of factors, including weather, crop disease, or pests. The weather in 1852, for instance, was unpredictable. After two or three weeks of spring-like weather in February and March, frost killed the early vegetation. Frosts continued into April. Though the weather remained cool, the rainfall was light so that by mid-June, the crops were in desperate need of rain. In the spring of 1854, the farmers experienced the opposite. Heavy rains damaged the corn, cotton, and wheat. The early spring of 1856 was warm with sufficient rain, but the weather turned dry in late spring.[17] In July of that year, Pisgah farmer Alexander Bell wrote his brother back in Carolina that he had "laid by" his corn about June 20. It looked good, despite the dry weather. Wheat crops were "not generally as good as the ware last year," Bell said. The week before, he had "thrashed out" 154 bushels of good wheat from the ten to twelve acres he had sowed. He had put in sixteen or seventeen acres of cotton. The lice had been on it, but he thought they were decreasing because the cotton had looked "more flurishing" during the last ten days.[18]

The crop season of 1857 got off to a bad start. One farmer called it "one of the most backward springs ever known" in Pope County. The winter lasted through April. In mid-April, the temperatures were ranging from the low thirties to the upper fifties. Written records claim that there was not a single peach in the entire state, and that after the trees had budded, a freeze came and froze the twigs on every tree for six inches below the leaves. It was not until after the third week in May that the leaves began to appear again, and it was thought for awhile that half of the timber was killed. By the middle of June the weather was pleasant with plenty of rain. Corn and cotton were both small but looked good and promised a good crop if the fall came late. The oat crop was fine. The wheat, which had been frozen to the ground, came out and was considered one of the best crops ever raised in the state, which the farmer expected to bring two dollars per hundred pounds.[19]

The uncertainty of farming results was constant. In the spring of 1858, Nancy Dickey wrote to Mary Ann McGill, "This spring has been warm and wet and corn and other things apear to gro hear fast we are planting corn at this time."[20] The next year, corn and cotton crops were fine, but rust infected the oats again and farmers feared they would lose them. The 1860 season did not look good, however. Heavy rains in early April had kept the streams swollen, but by early May the weather had turned "remarkably dry." Cyrus Ewing gathered from the newspapers that there would be a great failure of the wheat crop "everywhere," and that a scarcity of breadstuffs in Texas was causing an out migration from there. He had just paid $16.50 for two barrels of flour at Norristown, the highest he had known flour to be since he had been in Arkansas.[21]

Just as success in raising cotton, as other crops, varied from season to season, whether it netted the farmer ready cash depended on additional factors such as prices, shipping costs, or the level of the river. Cotton harvested in the fall was held until the following spring, normally the high-water season, when it was shipped by steamboat to New Orleans. The late winter and early spring of 1852 was a bad season on the river. The *Jefferson*, for instance, left Napoleon on January 10. On February 14, twelve miles below Dardenelle, it struck a snag, which knocked a hole in the bottom. The boat sank in only six feet of water, but she was so broken, it was "impossible to raise her." In testimony before Justice David Wells at Hog Thief Bend, it was determined that Master C. Rice, the other officers, and the crew had not been negligent and the loss and damages should be borne by the owners.[22]

The river was down all that season, and only one or two boats had run by May. Thus J. R. Homer Scott could not get his cotton shipped to New Orleans. In addition, the price of cotton was low. He wrote, "I fear much that cotton will not advance much more this season. I lost about two thousand last year on it, hope I shall sustain none this." He was probably saved, however, for a few days later the river "boomed."[23]

The 1855 season marked the beginning of a long time of low water. By June 1, 1856, Pope Countians were looking for the June rise. Without it, navigation would have been suspended for nearly two years, the longest time within the memory of the oldest residents. In the summer of 1856, however, Pisgah farmer Alexander Bell reported that he had shipped his previous year's crop to New Orleans the year before, "tho at a heavy expence and it neated me three hundred and 36 dollars." In 1857, depressed prices made Scott, a cotton buyer, reluctant: "The cotton crops are very fine but it is down to nothing almost. I lost two thousand dollars last spring on my cotton and I am afraid to buy it."[24]

Just as the river often determined whether the farmers had ready cash to spend, it also helped determine the availability and cost of goods they purchased. Merchants depended on the river for retail products. In May 1852 Scott wrote that he was waiting for the river to rise, hoping it would come in the next few days so the *Moses Greenwood* could "come from above" and Scott could board her for New Orleans. The local merchants were also waiting so that they could go down and "lay in goods."[25]

In letters to relatives and friends back in the Carolinas, the Pisgah settlers frequently spoke of the prices of store-bought goods. In 1854, for example, Thomas M. Oates wrote Alexander Weir that flour was three to four and one-half cents a pound, sugar was ten to twelve pounds to the dollar, molasses forty to fifty cents a gallon, salt $2.50 a sack; "that is in the stores here." Things could be bought for less by sending the order to New Orleans, he said. That, of course, depended on the river level. Alexander Bell wrote his brother on July 8, 1856, "Good flower is selling in our neighbourhood from 2 and a half to three dollars per hundred. groceries are high this year. as for corn and bacon, no call for it yet."[26]

The Pisgah settlers were, in fact, at the mercy of the river throughout the decade as the major means of shipping products, purchasing goods, or traveling. In 1854, Thomas Oates had held out the promising prospects of a railroad's passing near Pisgah as a means of enticing other settlers to the region. Considerable speculation would go on about the proposed Little Rock and Fort Smith Railroad. It was not until 1857, however, that any rails were laid toward rail service between Little Rock and Memphis. "I did send you last mail a paper," wrote Scott to his brother, "showing the rails were being commenced laying on the Little Rock & Memphis R. R."[27] It would be even later that the work would begin between Little Rock and Fort Smith, and the railroad would not reach Pope County until well after the Civil War. Stage-line service did come, however. In 1858, C. C. Ewing of Norristown expressed pride that the stage line brought mail and passengers from California to Norristown in twenty-two days. He wrote to his sister, "You could come almost to our door by stage from any direction if you or your neighbors want to take a ride to California now a days you can come by us."[28] One recent study indicates that this lack of transportation and resulting lack of access to markets directly shaped the agricultural development of the county.[29]

The isolation and the losses he sustained by the whims of the river caused Dover entrepreneur J. R. Homer Scott to become sarcastic at times about his home community. In 1856, for example, he wrote, "We live on hog and hominy with a small prospect of soon being out of sugar, coffee, and many of the essential comforts of life and worst of all nearly out of that ungodly peace blasting, soul absorbing, contentment killing article *Money*." His "hog and hominy" referred to the connection between the major crop and livestock productions in Pope County. It had become almost a refrain for Scott. In 1852, for example, he invited his relatives in Illinois to visit: "We will give them Ark. fare and a hearty welcome, 'Bacon, Beans or Hog & Hominy' as the case may be but none of the luxuries of life save the best milk and butter in the world."[30]

Scott's last statement gives away his sarcasm and indicates that the local diet was more diverse than "hog and hominy." A good indication comes from the 1860 agricultural census. Most Pisgah farm households raised both Irish and sweet potatoes, the latter in far greater quantities, however, than the former. Eliza E. Oates, for example, raised only nine bushels of Irish potatoes but one hundred of sweet. Alex Bell raised one hundred bushels of sweet potatoes but no Irish. Huge quantities of peas and beans were also produced: for example, J. R. McElwee, one hundred bushels; and Silas R. Parker, twenty-five. Butter production was also high. A. N. Falls processed one hundred pounds and Thomas M. Oates, sixty-eight.

For "sweetners" some Pisgah settlers maintained beehives: for example, Margaret M. Bigham and Thomas M. Oates each produced thirty pounds of honey. Others produced sorghum: Joseph D. Oates, for example, five gallons, and Alex Bell, twenty-four. They also gleaned the forest and prairie lands for wild plants for food and medicinal purposes, harvesting mullein, sassafras root, sumac berries, and poke salet. They used sunflower seeds and parched rye for "coffee" when the real article was in short supply.[31]

There was also a developing fruit culture. In 1858, Pisgah settler Nancy Dickey wrote to Mary Ann McGill that "fruit is plenty here this Season. . . . We have a orchard on this place and have fruit trees of all sorts in it."[32] On August 21, 1858, J. R. Homer Scott wrote his brother: "At this time having an abundance of the finest apples, peaches, melons & ere long will have some of the finest yams imaginable all of which added to our tame & wild turkeys, venison, Shanghais, and extra cured ham will inevitably conduce to a continuation of our present good health. Every day produces a fine peach 'cobbler' and a large bowl of peaches and cream." The peach crop was so good, in fact, that Scott conceived a plan to ship peaches north for sale.[33]

Scott's comments indicate that a considerably wider choice than "hog" made up the meat diet. Besides pork, beef, mutton, and domestic fowl, there was wild game: "Sam occasionally brings in from one to 5 & 6 young 'turkeys' before breakfast," Scott wrote. "Andrew has killed several squirrels." According to Molly Sinclair Falls, the meat diet was beef, mutton, pork, and wild game. "We had lots of squirrels," she said. "Fish was not depended on for supply."[34]

Evidence suggests that the Pisgah settlers during the 1850s were in many ways self-sufficient and enjoyed a growing prosperity. A profile of a "large" farm and a small one might serve as examples. Eliza E. Oates, for example, in 1860 reported 130 improved and 310 unimproved acres, valued at $6,600. She had two horses, five mules, eight milk cows, four oxen, twenty other cows, thirty sheep, and forty swine. She produced 214 bushels of wheat, 960 of corn, and 146 of oats. She also reported twenty-five bales of cotton, one hundred pounds of wool, ten bushels of peas or beans, nine of Irish potatoes, and one hundred of sweet potatoes, 156 pounds of butter, four tons of hay, one hundred and fifty dollars' worth of animals slaughtered for consumption, and two hundred dollars' worth of home manufactures. On a smaller scale, Franklin R. Bell had 30 acres of improved land valued at $300. He reported three horses, two milk cows, two other cows, eight sheep, fifty swine, forty-four bushels of wheat, four hundred of Indian corn, one hundred and fifty of oats, four bales of cotton, ten pounds of wool, seven bushels of Irish potatoes, twenty-five of sweet, twenty pounds of butter, two tons of hay, twenty-five dollars' worth of home manufactures, and thirty-five dollars' worth of animals slaughtered.[35] The population of Pope County in 1860 was 7,832, of which 957 were slaves.[36]

Though the vast majority of Pisgah people made their living by farming, there were some who, by the late 1850s, were engaged in other occupations. James G. Ferguson was a carpenter. Thomas L. Ferguson, James P. Ferguson, and James M. Henry were merchants. Franklin Raymond and John M. Ferguson were teachers. Alexander W. Henry was a physician, trained at Nashville University. Thomas Falls was a blacksmith, Silas Parker a mill owner and merchant, Henry Hill a stone mason, and Robert Ferguson a millwright. Some of these men also engaged in limited farming on the side.[37]

The best evidence of the prosperity of the Pisgah people at the end of the 1860s was their land holdings. They had come to Arkansas seeking land. Land prices rose steadily during the decade so that by 1858 some good land sold for more than twenty dollars an acre. "The Emigration has been so great the reason land is becoming valuable," wrote one prominent citizen. An outside observer who visited Galley Rock in 1858 for the first time in five years claimed that during his absence, prices had gone from $1.25 to $3 an acre to $10 to $40. The Pisgah covered-wagon settlers accounted for a good bit of the population growth and saw the value of the land they owned increase dramatically. They were still buying or selling land in 1860, when they bought or sold 1,302 acres. Of that, 1,182 acres sold for $10,152.50, or an average of $8.59 per acre. Sixty-six percent of heads of households in Pope County did not own land in 1860.[38] Households of the Pisgah people did not fit this pattern. Of fifty-eight heads of households identified in Illinois and Galley Rock townships, fifty-three owned land. These fifty-three held 11,268 acres at a combined value of $113, 255. Tax records for that year indicated that James Dickey owned the most land of any head of household: 1,710 acres.[39] He had about the same number of acres as wealthy Galley Rock planter, Ben T. Embry, although Embry's bottom land was more valuable. Another resemblance between Dickey and Embry was that their land values exceeded the value of their slaves, something that did not prevail among some landowners.

One indicator of wealth in the 1850s was the number of slaves, which constituted not only a labor resource but a capital asset. One recent history of Pope County argues that slave ownership provided a better index to economic status than land because land was cheap and the labor supply was limited.[40] In 1860, thirty-three of fifty-eight Pisgah households were slaveholding, the numbers owned ranging from one to twenty-four, the latter held by Silas R. Parker. Besides Parker, only Thomas Faulkner and Eliza E. Oates owned more than ten, suggesting a relationship between slave ownership and the substantial productivity of the Oates farm. Twenty-one owned fewer than five, with nine of those owning only one. Slave property figured prominently in the value of personal property held by the Pisgah households, which totaled $285,207.[41]

Tax records indicate other forms of wealth. In 1860, James Dickey of Galley Creek held taxable property in the amount of $12,132. In addition, Dickey had $3,000 loaned out and was collecting interest. The estate of John Oates IV, who had died in 1858, is also indicative. His estate had loaned out $5,000. Oates had already given strong backing to help his six older sons get started in life. He had also given some help to two daughters, and still more help to daughter Margaret Bigham, who lived in his home. After all this, he still had an estate whose value on the tax records was $11,890. Adding the $5,000 brought the total of the estate to $16,890.[42]

One final characteristic of the Pisgah people contributed to the economic success of their community and set them apart from the rest of Pope County's population: the practically total literacy of the adult community. Approximately 30 percent of the adult population of the county was illiterate in 1850, but practically all of the Pisgah settlers who came in the early 1850s were literate. One recent study of Pope County in the 1850s reported 100 percent literacy among the adult male population the study identified with Pisgah Church.[43] Like Calvinists before them, they believed in the necessity of reading the word of God in the practice of their religion. The church required its ministers to be educated and admonished its members to instruct their households in church beliefs and practices. That the Pisgah settlers owned books is evidenced in wills. Henry Taylor Sr., whose descendants migrated to Pope County, left a Bible, Psalm book, and dictionaries to his children in 1845. John Oates

IV specifically mentioned books in his will, and of A. N. Falls it was written: "He loved to read the Bible and the writings of old authors such as Knox."[44] The number of extant letters from Falls and others during the 1850s testifies to their literacy, which then, as now, was an element of economic advantage.

The economic status of the Pisgah community at the end of the 1860s is a testimonial to the determination of the first waves of covered-wagon settlers who arrived by 1855. By that time, they had achieved two major goals. The first was the establishment of an economic base for their families, a base that would provide for the general well-being of the group. The second was the establishment of a church, a church of course with an educated minister. These bases throughout the second half of the decade provided the incentive for further migrations and the continued growth of the church and the economy until the outbreak of the Civil War interrupted their flourishing way of life.

# ❊ Chapter 5 ❊

# "Carolina" in Pope County

Studies have indicated that kinship and previous community ties determined settlement patterns in Arkansas in the nineteenth century. Such conclusions are verified by the Pisgah community in Pope County, which continued to grow throughout the 1850s. By 1860, 1,002 persons, slightly more than 14 percent of the county's population, were from the Carolinas. Twenty-eight percent of residents in Illinois Township were from that region. In Galley Rock Township, in which resided 8 percent of the county's population, 31 percent of the free residents were of Carolina origin. A little less than one-fourth of the county's white population lived in Illinois and Galley Rock townships, and a little more than one-half of the county's residents listing the Carolinas as birth state lived there. On July 8, 1856, Alexander Bell, in a letter to his brother, said that the Pisgah settlement was called "Carolina."[1] It was a designation the Pisgah people not only liked, but one in which they took great satisfaction and pride because it connected them with their heritage. By the mid-1850s, the great migrations out of the Pisgah and Bethany communities in the Carolinas were over, but the Carolinians had already begun to revolutionize the economy of one of the most productive districts of Pope County. During the remainder of the decade, others would join them, not in vast numbers as previously, but in sufficient numbers to ensure the continued growth of the Pisgah community and church, both of which would be at the height of their prosperity on the eve of the Civil War.

The Carolina Pisgah-Bethany people were no doubt curious about the land their Carolina kin had settled in Arkansas. Just as there were visitors from Tennessee, there must have been a number of North and South Carolina people who also came for a visit to look over the land and its prospects. One such visit occurred in the winter of 1855–56, when James Dickey, Edwin Wilson, John Wilson, William Falls, Robert Ferguson, Thomas Ferguson, and James Ferguson "came to see the country."[2]

Without question, their motive, like that of their predecessors, was economic, but there may have been other reasons for their contemplated move. Earlier migrations from the vicinity of Pisgah Church in North Carolina, especially that of the Oates families, had depleted membership in the near vicinity of the church, and in 1855 it was moved.[3] Moving the church meant a shift in the community structure. It may have seemed an opportune time to relocate.

"Carolina" in Pope County expected another migration in the fall of 1856. Among those expected were Alexander D. Oates and Samuel B. Dickey, who wrote they were certain to come "if all is living and well." Some were looking for W. D. Hannah. Of Hannah and others, Alexander Bell wrote to his brother, "Wm. Falls told me that he said that he was a coming this fall; James Dickey's intention was when he left last Winter to moove this fall but he was taken sick on his way home last Winter and lay after he got home a long time he was able to walk up to Wm Fallses the last account and will cum if he is able and can get reddy, as for William Falls he didn't say what he intended to do but I think his intention is to come before long."[4]

As predicted, Samuel B. (1810–?) and Mary McGill Oates Dickey brought their family to Arkansas in 1856. Samuel was born in Lincoln County, North Carolina, the son of Alexander and Margaret (Blackwood) Dickey, his second wife. Dickey had come from Ireland or Scotland, and his wife was a native of North Carolina. Samuel B. was a half brother of Alexander Kidd Dickey, who came to Arkansas from Tennessee in 1854, and also of Margaret Dickey Oates, who came with her husband, William Oates, in 1851. Samuel's father-in-law, John Oates IV, had moved to Pope County in 1851. Mary Oates Dickey also had four brothers and two sisters in Arkansas. Now, she, her husband, and children Margaret, John O., Elizabeth J., and William joined the family in Arkansas.[5]

Whether James Dickey (1799–?), brother of Alexander K., had recovered sufficiently from his illness to emigrate to Arkansas in the fall is uncertain, but Ruth Bell Wharton thinks he, his wife, Mary, and daughters Susan, Mary, and Elizabeth came "about 1856," while sons Andrew J. and Alexander remained in Gaston County. As families often migrated together, it would seem a reasonable assumption that they may have come with Samuel Dickey and his family.[6]

From York District of South Carolina, two more families joined the

Pope County movement. The Josiah Henry and Andrew Kerr Henry families came to Arkansas together. Included in the group were Josiah (1792–1858) and Ann McElwee Henry (1795–1865) and their children, Alexander W., Mary M., and Josiah; Andrew Kerr (1812–1898) and Elizabeth Parker Henry (1819–1894) and their five children; and, perhaps, Elizabeth Henry's brother, Allison Parker (1823–1858). With the Andrew Henry party were six slaves.[7]

The Henrys were originally from the Lowlands, Firth of Forth, Scotland but had migrated to Ireland. William Henry Sr., born there in 1715, left his father's home at the age of seventeen and came to America, settling in Virginia.[8] About 1754 he and his family moved to what is now York District, South Carolina, near the mountain which bears the name of Henry's Nob; there he reared ten children. When hymns were introduced into worship at Long Creek and Beersheba Presbyterian churches, William, Alexander, and James Henry were among those who came out of those churches and helped form Old Kings Mountain Church. When two daughter churches were formed—Pisgah for those on the north side of Kings Mountain and Bethany for those on the south side of the mountain—the Henrys were among the prime movers in organizing Bethany Associate Reformed Presbyterian Church. The Henrys were prominent in the Revolutionary War and were instrumental in delaying the couriers from Maj. Patrick Ferguson to Lord Cornwallis, thus preventing British reinforcements at Kings Mountain.[9]

The Henrys made the trek of six weeks to Arkansas in covered wagons, four of which belonged to Andrew K. Henry. The campfires at night warded off wild animals, but away from the fires they heard the wolves howl and the panthers scream. Bears were more plentiful in those days, and the travelers included much bear meat in their diet. There was no traveling on the Sabbath; it was observed as a day of rest and worship. "His teams profited by the rest and he actually reached his destination ahead of those who were too eager to stop on Sundays," so write two Henry family historians. The trip was not easy. The rainy season overtook them. In the Mississippi bottoms, they spent two days prying the black mud of the swamps from the wheels, and a team was lost in the swamps. The Henrys arrived in December. Until better arrangements could be made, they had to live in their covered wagons.[10]

Friends helped them with corn and hay for their stock and with many other things. Among those they knew well was William McElwee, who came to Pope County in 1853, a friend of the family. The Henrys and the McElwees had probably been family friends as far back as County Tyrone, Ireland, and later, Virginia, and had lived nearly one hundred years together on the South Carolina frontier. Ann McElwee Henry, wife of Josiah Henry Sr., was the daughter of famed American Revolutionary soldier James McElwee. Elizabeth Serenia Parker Henry, wife of Andrew K. Henry, was the daughter of Silas R. and Martha Akin Parker, of Union County, South Carolina. She and her brother, Allison, would prove to be the vanguard of members of the Parker family to move to Arkansas. More Henrys would also come to Pisgah community in later years. One of the most notable was Margaret Kerr Henry, widow of William and mother of Andrew Kerr Henry. Her husband died in the Carolinas in 1848. When son Alexander M. came to Pisgah in the early 1870s, Margaret, then eighty-five, came with him. She lived to be ninety-eight, dying in 1888, and was buried in Pisgah Cemetery.[11]

In 1857 the migrations continued. In the summer and early September, four families in Lincoln County, Tennessee, prepared for the move: the families of Henry M. Hughey, Jonathan Pinkerton, James Isam Allbright, and Franklin Raymond, who left Lincoln County the last of September. It appears that the Hughey party included Henry M. and Rebekah Pinkerton Hughey (1820–1885) and children Hiel, Sarah Jane, John, Isaac, Martha, James W., Lemuel H., and Mary E.[12] The Hugheys, like other families who had supplied descendants for the Pisgah community, had ancestors who had left Scotland because of religious conflict and in the early 1700s migrated to Ireland and finally to Pennsylvania in search of better soil and climate and a place where they could "have a church of their own in which they could worship as their spirits dictated." They arrived in the midst of the French and Indian War and "found life among the trappers and warriors so different from their own that they again pulled up stakes and moved into North and South Carolina," setting down roots at last in Lincoln County, North Carolina; "those stalwart, ever enduring families saw the construction of their own original Pisgah Associate Reformed Presbyterian Church, and across the line of South Carolina, the Bethany Reformed Presbyterian Church." The Hugheys, like the Dickeys and Sinclairs, who had migrated to Arkansas before them, were among the people from Lincoln County, North Carolina, who had later gone to

Tennessee, where Henry M. was born December 16, 1812, near Fayetteville. He married Rebekah Pinkerton on September 1, 1836.[13]

Also in the 1857 party from Lincoln County, Tennessee, were Rebekah Hughey's brother Johnathan (1809–1879) and his wife, Elizabeth Sloan Pinkerton (1805–1881), and children Martha and John C. Johnathan and Rebekah were the children of James Pinkerton of Camden District, South Carolina, and Elizabeth Sloan Pinkerton was a native of either Fairfield or Chester counties, but spent the greater part of her life in Lincoln and Marshall counties, Tennessee, where she was a devout member of the Associate Reformed Presbyterian Church. It was said of her life in Pope County, "Although living at an inconvenient distance from the church, and not being permitted to attend its services as frequently as desired, she enjoyed the ordinances of God's house, and was rarely absent from a Communion."[14]

Two other families came in the migration from Lincoln County. The family of Franklin Raymond, a teacher and native of Massachusetts, came with his wife, Jennette, a native of South Carolina, and children Catherine and Griselda. The Allbright family included James Isam (1825–?), a native of Lincoln County, his wife, Martha, a native of Virginia, and their daughters. The original destination of the Hugheys, Allbrights, Pinkertons, and Raymonds was Yell County, Arkansas. They traveled in five wagons pulled by oxen and one wagon and surrey with horses for the women and children. The eyes of the people in the caravan became wide at Memphis, where for the first time, they saw a train depot, train, locomotive, and roundhouse. They crossed the Mississippi River by steamboat and picked their way with extreme care through the swampy bottoms. They crossed the St. Francis and White rivers on ferries and went on to Little Rock, where they turned northward. After four weeks' travel, they reached Pope County in the last part of October. One mile east of Russellville, they made camp on the prairie. After firmly establishing the women and children in camp, the men set out to their original destination, Yell County. They explored the country for a week but found the country "very unfavorable," as one family member put it. The men returned, declaring they would not take their families into Yell County because the people there looked sick unto death. The Hugheys bought land west and the Allbrights south of Russellville, the Hugheys later moving to Bradley's Cove. There they built a large log house and reared their family.[15]

There may have been other reasons for their staying in Pope County which no one suggested. The people at Pisgah and Bethany, hearing of their arrival and some of them knowing the Hugheys as far back as Pisgah Church in North Carolina, may have insisted they stay in Pope County. Then, again, the recently arrived travelers from Tennessee knew the Sinclairs and Dickeys, not only from Pisgah, but also in Tennessee.

The fall of 1857 apparently brought another caravan from the Carolinas: the Faulkner family from South Carolina and perhaps another Oates family from North Carolina. The Pisgah, Arkansas, Session records, where this supposition originates, were vague on the matter, for Monroe Oates does not pinpoint the exact year. The Faulkners had been early settlers near the Waxhaw Creek, Mecklenburg County, North Carolina. Thomas Faulkner (1801–?) was born in Lancaster County, South Carolina, the son of Thomas and Agnes McElwee Faulkner, the latter the daughter of William McElwee and Janet Black. Widowed shortly after the birth of their son, Agnes returned to the Bethany community in York County and lived with her widowed sister, Eleanor McElwee Leslie, until she died in early 1856. Members of her son's family who migrated were Thomas and his wife, Nancy Kincade Faulkner (1804–?), and probably their children William J., James P., Margaret L., Alex T., and Sarah A. Also in his party were perhaps as many as eleven slaves.[16] They settled in Illinois Township near the Andrew Kerr Henry family. They were also close to the home of Ann B. McElwee Henry. Other neighbors were Elizabeth B. McElwee, and her son William L. and his family. There was another McElwee in the same neighborhood, William McElwee, who must have been looked on as the patriarch of these families, indeed as a patriarch of the Pisgah-Bethany community.

There were other arrivals in 1857. In the same caravan with the Faulkners may have been Alexander D. (1828–1883) and Mary Oates (1827–1873) and their children Jane, Andrew, John, and Sarah, adding to the large number of others of the same family that had already settled in Pope County. Also in the group may have been William Millen and Isabella Faulkner Galloway and children William, Louisa, Thomas, Nancy, and Margaret. They came from Yorkville, South Carolina, arrived on November 20, 1857, and located at Norristown three miles south of Russellville.[17] Galloway was descended from Alexander Galloway Sr., a weaver who was born in Ireland in 1746 and settled in Lancaster, South

Carolina, where he was a soldier in the American Revolution, fighting in the battle of Kings Mountain. William was the son of Alexander Jr. and Mary McElwee Galloway of York County, and his wife was the daughter of Thomas and Nancy Kincade Faulkner.[18] In 1884, Monroe Oates wrote of the Pisgah Church, "In 1857 the following accessions were received from Lincoln County, Tennessee—Mr. Franklin Raymond, H. M. Hughey and Johnathan Pinkerton, and from Smyrna, South Carolina Mr. Thomas Falkner and perhaps Mr. W. R. Chesnut from Cobb County, Georgia."[19] Chesnut's family included his wife, Susanan, and children George, Frances, Jane, Susan, and John S. Chesnut was chosen elder at Pisgah in 1858, but he did not serve long, for by 1859 he had moved on to Fulton County.

Three families arrived in Pisgah in 1858: the Parkers, the McArthurs, and the Anthonys. The domino effect on the emigration of families is seen in the Silas R. (1788–1867) and Martha Akin Parker (1796–1860) family of York County, South Carolina. Of their nine children, the oldest two, Allison and Elizabeth, wife of Andrew K. Henry, had preceded them to Arkansas in 1856. With Parker were apparently Peter W. and Mary Parker, L. W. Parker, William R. Parker, Sarah Alexander, and S. B. Alexander. They traveled by wagon, bringing perhaps thirty slaves and settled south of Pottsville, where Parker built a gristmill and store on Galley Creek. Exactly when Silas and Martha A. Parker arrived in 1858 is uncertain, but they were there by May, when Parker sold five of his slaves.[20]

Sometime in 1858, John C. McArthur and his family migrated to Pope County.[21] Some of the McArthur family were already in Pope County. Isabella, the daughter of Joseph and Martha Montgomery McArthur, had married Robert Quinn, and they and their children John W. and Sarepta N. had migrated from South Carolina about 1856. Also in Pope County, apparently since at least 1857, were Joseph M. McArthur and his wife, Nancy. In the McArthur party in 1858 were Isabella McArthur Quinn's siblings Mattie D. (1840–1905), who married Peter W. Parker, William C., and A. W. Another daughter Hannah would follow. She and her husband, William Anthony, were members of Pisgah Church, North Carolina, where their daughter Martha Elizabeth was baptized in September 1858, shortly before they left for Yell County, Arkansas.[22]

William and Hannah McArthur Anthony made the trip from North Carolina, taking three months to get as far as Rover in Yell County. Flooding on the river forced them to camp at Fourche near there, where

William became ill, died, and was buried. Hannah Haw Lewis Scott writes, "Before William died he begged Hannah to take the little daughter and go back to Carolina." But when the water receded, Hannah went on to Pope County, where they had planned to go before they left Carolina, where she joined other members of her families, made a home for her daughter, and later married Samuel Wells.[23]

By 1859, migrations from the Carolinas had all but ceased, though an occasional immigrant arrived during the next two years to join relatives. Four years earlier, for instance, the Reverend John Patrick had brought his new wife, Mary E., to Pisgah. She was the daughter of John and Sarah Patrick of Union County, South Carolina. Her brother Hiram Patrick had probably come with them and was living in Pope County. Her sister Sarah A. migrated with her husband, William Marion Peeler, in the fall of 1859, and they lived for a time with the Patricks in their log home in the Cove. In late 1860 Mary Ann Blackwood Daniels went to Pope County from Wayne County, Tennessee, after the death of her husband. Her sister Margaret, wife of Gregory Sinclair, had been in the Pisgah community for a number of years. Their grandfather, James Blackwood, had been a trustee of Pisgah Church in Gaston County, North Carolina. Mrs. Daniels brought her two children, Jasper M. and Margaret E., and gave birth to Amanda P. after she arrived in Arkansas.[24]

The migrations ceased for a number of reasons, but foremost may have been that economic opportunities began to flag. Opportunity had underpinned the great Pisgah migrations of the 1850s. The patriarchs brought their families, not because they did not have land or homes or money, and neither did they come because they were not culturally integrated in their home communities of Pisgah and Bethany in the Carolinas. They were leaders in these communities as revealed by the church membership rolls of that time at old Long Creek Presbyterian Church and at Beersheba and later Pisgah and Bethany Associate Reformed Presbyterian churches. Like these people, the satellite immigrants who came from Lincoln County, Tennessee, were leaders. They were not the big plantation owners; they were the respected country gentry who formed one of the most solid backbone groups of the Scots-Irish immigrants. They had added their numbers to the rapidly expanding population of Pope County, which diminished the availability of fertile land to be had.

Migrations to Pisgah also declined because of the decreasing numbers of close family ties in the Carolinas. The early migrations had contained the heads of large extended families, whose members came directly or migrated in later years. Now the patriarchs and matriarchs of those families were passing from the scene: John and Elizabeth Oates Falls, John Harbison, Josiah Henry, John Oates IV, Jane McElwee. With each passing, ties to the old communities in the Carolinas were broken.

It had been at least eighteen years since the first members of the North Carolina Pisgah community migrated to Pope County. In 1842, James Bradley and John Willson began trying to lure their old friends, the Alexander Weir family, to Arkansas. After the large migrations from Pisgah-Bethany in the early 1850s, Andrew Nael Falls had tried to get the Weirs to migrate, and in 1854 Thomas Oates had had his try at them, all to no avail. In early 1859, Weir wrote his old friend Bradley, and his letter reveals the distance that both men now felt between their two communities. It reads like an account of affairs in a community unfamiliar to the reader, much like the accounts of life in Arkansas that newly arrived immigrants in former days had written back to Weir.

He began almost poetically about the changes that had come about in old Lincoln (now Gaston) County since Bradley had left: "I suppose if you or any of your family could be transported and set down some dark night on Crowders Crek when day would brake in uppon you how supprised would you be to see how man and things change in the short space of fifteen or twenty years our County vilage improves slowly but shourly Their is but few very interprising men doing business their their is three stoars doing a tolarable business and two starved grocers. . . . times are hard and produce low." Later he writes, "Step over and see what a fine house is now raising in the Linzy's [Lindsey's] old field besides many others on the sandy rigis [ridges] round about us."

The economy occupied much of Weir's concern. In giving the price of goods, he listed "flower," corn, and "poark," and added money, about which he wrote, "exceedingly scarse with a greate demand for it." He was concerned that more deeds of trust had been made in the last twelve months in his "cuntry" than had been made in the preceding thirty years: "a greate many men who stood fair and was looked uppon as the welthy of the land who fall far short of their liabilities the honest industrious farmer has to loose his hard ernings through these unrighteous Deeds of trust friend Bradley if I could see you face to face I could entertain you with many stories of the past which I forbair wrighting."[25]

His own "cropping" on Crowder's Creek had produced two to three hundred bushels of wheat and four to six hundred of corn. The most likely market was at Briggs Iron Works, a "greate market" for the neighborhood "in the corn line of business if he onely can hoald out and still pay." It was also the market for what else the farmer "can spair."

Weir caught Bradley up on the general health and mortality of families that he knew—Bradley, Sarvis, and McNair—and seemed nostalgic about his friends in the west. He asked James to tell John M. Bradley, James's oldest son, "I would be glad to read a letter from him." Many letters had been lavished on Weir over the years in an attempt to get him to emigrate, perhaps because he himself had held out the possibility that he might do so. And, now, after so many years of separation, he still cherished the hope of one time seeing his friends in Arkansas: "I still though[t] at some time not far distant that would see that cuntry I no not what will turn up."[26] If Weir, in turn, could have been transported to Pope County some dark night, the light of daybreak would have revealed to him many of those who, by emigrating from Gaston County, had wrought the changes on the Pope County landscape that he spoke about in his own community and who had reformed themselves into a prosperous community in the west.

The nucleus of that community was Pisgah Church, which had grown steadily as a result of the large migrations and which was conducted according to familiar, long-standing practice. The third week in May was Communion season. On Thursday and Friday were held Preparatory Services, and on the Sabbath, Communion. That day, elders were elected, and new members received into the congregation. In 1856, Hugh Taylor was elected elder to serve with Alexander Dickey, James Quinn, Andrew N. Falls, John Oates IV, and John Oates V. Though it had lost John Falls, one of the original elders, in death, the young congregation was building a strong session. In 1857, nine members, who had previously appeared before the session, were received, eight by certificate and one by examination,[27] an indication that most members were recently arrived immigrants from the south. The new members, who were welcomed into the fellowship of Pisgah Church, were reminded by the Reverend Patrick of their privileges, duties, and responsibilities to the body of Christ. The new member who had come by examination would join in the taking of the bread and the cup for the first time.

That year, the Synod of the South placed the work in Arkansas under the inspection of the Memphis Presbytery. This presbytery, organized in 1853, had been composed of churches in west Tennessee and northern Mississippi.[28] Besides Pisgah and the church at Monticello, organized in 1855, there were growing Associate Reformed Presbyterian communities as well in Drew, Bradley, and Fulton counties.

In 1858, membership in the Pisgah Church showed a dramatic increase. On May 22, the session received twenty-four members, nineteen by certificate and five by examination, bringing the membership to "one hundred or more." About this time, though the date is uncertain, Franklin Raymond, Thomas Faulkner, and W. R. Chesnut were chosen elders.[29] The date seems likely because all of these men had migrated to Pisgah the year before.

Pisgah community was visited that early fall by the Reverend Monroe Oates, who preached not only at Pisgah but also at Prosperity community in Fulton County and in Drew and Hempstead counties. Oates was the son of John Oates IV, who had been an elder at Pisgah in North Carolina and at Pisgah in Pope County. The younger Oates had remained in the east to continue his education instead of emigrating with his family, graduating from Erskine College in 1855 and completing the course in theology at Due West, South Carolina, in 1858. He was licensed by the Second Presbytery on September 7, after which he departed for Arkansas and went back east to continue his mission work.[30]

Throughout this period of tremendous growth, the Reverend John Patrick's appointment had been renewed on a year-by-year basis. In 1860 his appointment ended, the synod in the fall of 1859 appointing the Reverend J. L. McDaniel as missionary.[31] McDaniel was delayed because of bad weather and the swamps west of the Mississippi until the spring. He preached twice in St. Francis County where four Associate Reformed families lived. He preached ten Sabbaths at Pisgah and "three other places." He reported the church at Pisgah in a very prosperous condition, God's people renewed through the Communion Service, which he conducted before he left. The preaching began on Friday, and "the hearts of God's people were much revived," he wrote. "Twenty-one persons were received into the church by examination, and three by letter."[32] Only one of those received is known: Sarah Patrick Peeler, sister-in-law of the Reverend John Patrick. The total membership was about 125. James McElwee was elected elder. By then, Elders John Falls Sr., John Oates IV, and John Oates V had died, and W. R. Chesnut had removed to Prosperity in Fulton County, where he became a leader in the church established there.[33]

The Reverend McDaniel, who remained several months at Pisgah, pleased the church, which apparently sent a request for his services. He had urged the synod to station missionaries in various parts of Arkansas. "That is a pretty country," he wrote; "the field is an inviting one, and now is the right time to send missionaries there.—Many souls in that country are exceedingly glad to hear the word of God preached." Of Pisgah he had said, "She embraces nearly forty families, is ripe for settlement, and ought to have a regular Pastor," though he did not want to return there himself and asked to remain with the Memphis Presbytery.[34] Thus in the fall, the synod sent twenty-three-year-old David Kerr (1837–1874) to labor in Arkansas, to spend the greater part of his time at Pisgah. The son of Jennings B. and Jane Walkup Kerr, he had graduated from Erskine College at age twenty and then studied theology at Erskine Seminary. He was licensed by the Second Presbytery in August 1860 and that fall sent to Arkansas.[35] Because Pisgah was essentially a church of young people, the new young minister was no doubt a boost to them.

Though Pope County had been the main focus of migrations in the 1850s, there had been a growing diaspora of Associate Reformed Presbyterians in Arkansas. In December 1856, fifteen members of Neely's Creek Church left York County, South Carolina, and arrived three months later in Bradley County. The Monticello church had continued to grow, drawing mainly from Tipton County, Tennessee, and Chester County, South Carolina. An offshoot of that church, Mount Zion, was organized in 1858. In the summer of 1859, the Reverend J. M. Brown came to the Bradley County group and organized Hickory Springs Church with fifteen members and Johnathan Davis and J. F. Leslie as elders. Prosperity Church was organized by the Reverend W. S. Moffatt in Fulton County in 1859, with thirty-two charter members, largely from Tennessee and Georgia.[36] Elders were W. A. Gault and W. R. Chesnut, the latter of whom had migrated to Pope County from Georgia in 1857 and had been elected elder at Pisgah in 1858. His movement to Fulton County reflects the close family and geographical bonds that formed the web of these communities.

The year of 1861 dawned bright for Pisgah Church. It had grown from the approximately thirty charter members to more that 125. Its growth is more remarkable if compared to the number of members received in recent years in churches of the general synod of the Associate Reformed Presbyterian Church. How many rural churches today are even approaching the growth of Pisgah? There are two things to consider about its growth. Pisgah was receiving members because of the migrations. Second, the Pisgah families usually had a number of children. It must be considered that the fathers of the migrations were bringing their families to Pisgah mainly because they thought their children would have better opportunities in a new land on virgin soil. They also had every intention to provide for the worship of God as they understood it. As one writer about the church has written, "These people brought Pisgah Church in their hearts from the Carolinas. Used to Gospel privileges in their old homes, they must have them in their new. So the church was established among them after 'pitching camp.'"[37]

The growth continued in 1861. On Friday before the first Sabbath in May, the Reverends John Patrick, J. M. Brown, J. A. Dickson, W. S. Moffatt, and A. Mayn met at Pisgah and organized the Arkansas Presbytery to embrace the churches within the bounds of the state of Arkansas. On May 4, 1861, twelve new members were received by the church; the only one whose name is known was Calvin Grier Oates.[38] The elders in 1861 were Dr. F. Raymond, Alexander Dickey, Hugh Taylor, A. N. Falls, James Quinn, Thomas Faulkner, and James McElwee.

The Reverend Monroe Oates wrote of Pisgah as it was in 1861. "Pisgah was then in the midst of her prosperity," he said. "Her prospects were very bright at that time. She was strong, if she had known her strength. There were many well to do families. Many worthy men and women in connection with the Church with promising children."[39] His comments reflect the unity and stability of the community. That stability is supported by the membership numbers cited by the Reverend McDaniel in 1860. The disproportionate number received by examination that year indicates that the older members, who brought their memberships by certificate from other congregations, were now fulfilling their family and church duty by rearing their children in church practice. Those children, like Calvin Grier Oates, for example, were now entering the church and far outnumbered those who were coming from other congregations.

Thus in 1861, the church and community were prospering. Prospects looked good. The Reverend David Kerr was returned by the synod that year, apparently "to the entire satisfaction of the church," Monroe Oates later wrote.[40] The prospects at Pisgah may have been as bright as any rural church in the Arkansas River Valley, but the "gathering storm" was getting closer to the Pisgah people. Before the year was out, they would be caught in the civil struggle that would not only rend the nation but debilitate the community.

# ❃ Chapter 6 ❃

# Pisgah in the Civil War

When the ministers met at Pisgah on May 3, 1861, to form the Arkansas Presbytery, the nation was literally on the verge of war. The election of Abraham Lincoln had been reason for some Arkansas politicians to begin a movement toward secession, though most citizens of the state did not think the election was sufficient cause to break the Union. However, a rising debate on secession, urged on by prominent politicians and others, resulted in a convention of delegates from seventy-three counties, who met in Little Rock in early 1861 to discuss the question. However, they failed to pass secession ordinances. Fort Sumter in South Carolina was fired upon on April 12; Lincoln called for volunteers. Both of these events increased the tensions all over the south. The debate in Arkansas continued, and on May 6, only three days after the historic meeting at the Pisgah Church, the secession convention reconvened in Little Rock. The convention voted for secession 69 to 1, the sole negative vote cast by Isaac Murphy of Huntsville. The convention created a military board to call for ten thousand volunteers and provided for a system of taxation to finance the war. This event was a harbinger of the military occupation of the Pisgah countryside; of the separation of families; of a terrible toll in lives of community members; of stealing, shooting, and looting; and of turning family against family. It was a prelude to animosities that would continue to be spoken of in the Pisgah community a hundred years later.

The idea of secession had been hotly debated in Pope County. As the election of 1860 approached, by far the most vocal support in the county had been for John Bell of Tennessee and the Constitutional Union party, ostensibly given in the name of preserving the Union. Black Republicans and secessionist Democrats, the argument ran, were both engaged in an effort to break the Union by continuing to agitate the question of slavery, which the Bell supporters argued was protected by the Constitution.[1] However, after Lincoln's election and state after state followed South

Carolina in seceding, the former "unionists" of Pope County began to move toward a secessionist position, albeit reluctantly they claimed.

In the wake of Arkansas's secession, J. R. Homer Scott of Dover wrote a sad but defiant letter to his brothers in the north. The slaveholding states had been deceived by Lincoln's policy, he said: "But the slave states now see that the design is to exterminate slavery, if it is to be done by the total annihilation of the Southern people." Scott had hoped for a constitutional resolution until the firing at Fort Sumter. After that, he was a rebel, he said, "to the bitter end." Scott wavered between regret and defiance. "Our once happy and glorious land," he said, "is to be converted into a land of Blood, and all the horrors of civil war. When father & son & brother & brother, shall be arrayed upon the battlefield in deadly conflict, in the work of annihilation. Great God; is there no barrier, no interposing power, to check & put down so unholy, so mad, & reckless an undertaking?" On the other hand, in defiance he said, "There is no dissenting voice, the State is out and united to a man, & every man woman & child ready to fight for the South. You never saw such a unity & determination to resist coercion at all hazards."[2]

Scott's assessment of unity was overstated to say the least. A good deal of pro-Union and antislavery sentiment existed in the county. After the war, for example, Cyrus C. Ewing, a Kentuckian who lived at Norristown and who had sold the Reverend John Patrick the land for his home, wrote to his sister, "You say you were in hope I would of stood neutral. I will tell you an honest man could not stand so down in the Devil's Dominion. He had to choose to be a robbing and plundering rebel or a friend to that good man Abraham Lincoln that God raised up to deliver the poor negroes from bondage."[3]

But there was, at least on the eve of secession, a division of opinion within Ewing's own household. His daughter Missouri wrote effusively and romantically to her aunt: "Aunt I must confess I differ greatly with you union. I am in favor of union as far as you, but the south cannot get her just rights in the Union. So I say Go Out. I think from your letter that you Kentucky folks are kind of submissive to all of the Lincoln operations. The thought of having a black Republican for a President is too much like putting ourselves on an equality with the negro. Mr. Lincoln thinks the negro his equal and soon we will have them witness against us in every case. So I think you will never stand that and at last come over with the South. Secession is gaining ground fast. Arkansas has not gone out yet. I sincerely hope and trust however soon it may. . . ."[4]

Unlike Missouri Ewing, the Pisgah community at large had not supported the idea of secession. In fact, as two community historians put it, speaking of the Oates family, "While the Civil War clouds were gathering and secession becoming increasingly an issue, they remained strict unionists."[5] Whether their views of the Union were shaped by the role that their progenitors had played in helping shape it is uncertain. Contention over the issues of the day, particularly states' rights and slavery, almost certainly reminded them of controversies many of them had been embroiled in in earlier years.

In the early decades of the century, the slavery issue had driven a wedge between the Associate Presbyterians and the Associate Reformed Church, causing many of the former to leave the south. When the Associate Synod of North America directed its members to free their slaves in 1831, the ruling drove many associate congregations back to the Associate Reformed Synod of the South, including those at Pisgah and Bethany in 1833. Their pastor, the Reverend Joseph Banks, ultimately found his views on slavery incompatible with those of these communities and went north. Slavery's twin issue, nullification, added to factionalism within the congregations.[6] According to Herbert Oates, the attitude of some of the Oates family toward slavery was so unacceptable at Pisgah in North Carolina that their crops were destroyed and their barns burned, and they, like Banks, departed for the north. Because of these recent events in their church's history, it is likely that the Pisgah people in Arkansas looked at the slavery debate preceding secession in a different light than did their Pope County neighbors.

There is reason to believe, in fact, that they may have looked at the institution of slavery differently from the way neighboring owners such as Ben T. Embry and Scott did. Though the Synod of the South is not known to have condemned slavery officially, it took what has been described as "a moderate position" on the issue.[7] Official church action was certainly out of step with prevailing practices in the south. In 1828 the Associate Reformed Synod had said that it was the master's duty to teach his servants to read the Bible. In 1838, it said that it was the duty of the session to require masters and heads of families to baptize their servants as well as their children.[8]

In 1845 the synod passed an act recognizing that slaves had souls and took action to shore up the institution of marriage among them. It resolved that owners should instruct their slaves regarding "the divine appointment of the nature and obligation of marriage" and encourage them to observe the formalities of marriage. The synod made it the owner's duty not to separate married slaves at "such a distance from each other as virtually to dissolve the marriage relation." If a church member owned one party in a marriage and a neighbor the other, the member was obligated "to adopt all fair, reasonable and honest measures" to prevent the neighbor from separating them. But if the neighbor persisted, the blame fell on him, not the member. If the member was the party whose action would effect the separation, the blame fell on him.[9]

To what extent the slaveholders at Pisgah conformed to these acts of synod is unknown. In view of their devotion to church duty in other matters, it seems likely that church policy had some impact on their attitudes toward their servants. Some evidence points in that direction. The ministers of the synod were clearly concerned about the spiritual well-being of slaves.[10] The session records of Pisgah Church, North Carolina, indicate that in 1850, a slave girl named Sarah, owned by John Oates, was baptized. Discrepancies between the number of slaves Pisgah members owned in the Carolinas and the number for which they were first taxed in Arkansas may not have resulted, in some cases, from mortality but from sale or other arrangements to leave slaves in the Carolinas to prevent family separation. Once in the west, slaveholders generally did not sell slaves. The absence of slave deeds for Pisgah people in the Pope County records is remarkable. Only Silas R. Parker is known to have sold slaves, and that shortly after his arrival in the west. Also, deeds of trust for slaves, made by some families years before removal to the west, kept slave families intact until the Civil War.[11] Finally, there is evidence of genuine concern for the welfare of slave individuals. John Falls, for example, upon his death in 1855, provided that "in case Sandy should get so that he cannot pay his expenses," Falls's son John F. "must take said negro man and take care of him."[12]

However humane, though, slavery was still involuntary servitude. Caring for a slave's well-being was quite separate from accepting the legality of the institution and the southern concept of the individual's right to hold chattel. Thus after secession, though a few of the staunchest people at Pisgah remained loyal to the Union cause, most were solidly behind the Confederate States of America. The Bell family was perhaps typical. Neill Bell wrote, "The Bell family, along with those of their group and, as for that matter, the State of Arkansas, endeavoured to avoid the conflict until the call for volunteers forced a decision."[13] This family would send six sons to the Confederate army.

The first stirrings leading to military action by Pisgah people came from Galla Rock through the efforts of Ben T. Embry, one of the most prominent citizens and probably the largest planter in the county. Embry may have started some military training in the spring of 1861, for by early summer he had organized what was later commonly called "Company B." Whether Embry and others believed, like many, that this would be a ninety days' war is uncertain. Calvin Grier Oates, a member of the unit, later said that he left home on July 7, perhaps the date the unit left for Osage Prairie near Bentonville, where, in late July, Company B, 2d Arkansas Regiment of Mounted Rifles, was mustered into Confederate service. Embry was captain, and, from Pisgah, Peter W. Parker was first lieutenant, William C. McArthur was first corporal, and John T. Falls was fourth corporal. Besides these, others from the Pisgah community belonging to this unit were William Beck; John M. Bell; William R. Clark; John O. Dickey; James P. and William J. Faulkner; James Q. and Thomas L. Falls; John M. Ferguson; Josiah W. and Silas A. Henry; Henry W. and Lawson R. Hill; Ephriam Hoffman; Heil F. Hughey; James H., Samuel B., and William L. McElwee; Calvin G., James A., John C., and Thomas M. Oates; and Eleazer D. Parker.[14] Though Company B was the unit that enlisted most of the men from Pisgah to serve the Confederacy, the list of its ranks does not tell the whole story. Others would serve in different Confederate units, and still others would serve in the Union army.

Company B quickly saw action, and reports of casualties soon began to arrive at Pisgah. Only days after it was organized, the regiment was ordered to march from Cassville, Missouri, toward Springfield, with Col. James McIntosh in command of the 2d Arkansas Mounted Rifles. Captain Embry was promoted to lieutenant colonel and placed second in command, and Lt. Peter Parker was promoted to captain of the company. At the Union victory at Wilson's Creek near Springfield, Missouri, on August 10, there were twenty-five hundred Union and Confederate casualties, among whom were six members of Company B: John R. B. Ford of Norristown, Joseph S. Bunker of Russellville, Edward F. Carroll and

John L. Sweeten from Point Remove Creek, and Lawson Hill of Pisgah, who had been living with the Alexander Oates family. Among the wounded were William E. Cleveland and Thomas L. Falls. After the battle, McIntosh wrote to General McCulloch, "My officers behaved in this first fight with great bravery and coolness," and he commended his captains, including Peter W. Parker, for the way they had led their companies.[15]

The list of casualties among the Pisgah men continued to grow in 1861. Some were apparently unrelated to battlefield action. On August 16, thirty-eight-year-old Robert Quinn died. Quinn, who had joined the Pisgah community in the mid-1850s, left his widow, Isabella, and children John, Sarepta, and Mary. On September 24, 1861, William L. McElwee, one of the original members of Company B, died. Though one source states he died in the battle of Wilson's Creek, he apparently died near home, perhaps of some epidemic that swept the forces. Also in 1861, Ephriam Hoffman, seventeen-year-old son of Peter and Ann Hoffman, was killed near Springdale. These deaths may be accounted for by the fact that the 2d Arkansas returned south after Wilson's Creek and went into winter quarters at Van Buren and at Spadra Bluff near Clarksville to avoid exposure to the smallpox epidemic at Fort Smith.[16]

Company B continued to see action. In December the 2d Arkansas was ordered to Fort Gibson, Indian Territory, and on December 26, it fought in the battle of Chustenalah against the Loyal Creek forces under Opothleyohola. William C. McArthur was wounded. On January 26, 1862, the regiment was reorganized. Command passed from James McIntosh to Ben T. Embry, who was promoted to colonel. In early March, Company B fought in the terrible battle at Pea Ridge, and, under Embry's command, suffered no deaths. However, Caleb Davis, Lorenz D. Love, Richard B. Minton, Calvin Grier Oates, and James A. Oates were captured, and Jacob Tiner was wounded.[17] Some of these either escaped or were paroled, for they appear on casualty lists later in the war.

In 1862, others left Pisgah to join the conflict. In February, another large group of Pisgah men enlisted for Confederate service. Company F, 1st Battalion, Arkansas Cavalry, was organized at Russellville, under Capt. John Randall. James G. Ferguson was third lieutenant, and among the enlisted men from Pisgah were Samuel Oates, William A. Bell, Robert H. Dickey, James M. Henry, William Oates, Joseph Oates, James W. Dickey, and John W. Ferguson. John Franklin Falls, who was engaged in the mercantile business at Parker's Mill, also volunteered for Confederate service sometime in 1862.[18]

Both Company B and Company F were among the troops transported east of the Mississippi in April 1862 and who saw battle in north Mississippi. The Pisgah community suffered its losses this time among the members of Company F. John Franklin Ferguson, twenty-year-old son of Robert A. Ferguson, was lost at Corinth in April 1862. On August 6, Joseph Dixon Oates (1823–1862) died of camp fever in Itawamba County, Mississippi. A son of John Oates IV, he had been in the advance scouting party that came to seek a suitable place for a colony in the Arkansas River Valley in 1850. He had married Nancy D. McElwee, daughter of William and Betsy McElwee, who had moved to Pope County in 1853. They settled on a farm about three miles south of Pottsville, where, during his absence in service, Nancy made the crops and reared their two little boys, Murray and Willie. He left her a widow to rear them alone. In Mississippi, a great hole was dug, and Joseph, along with other Confederate soldiers, was buried in it. Joseph's eighteen-year-old brother, Samuel Wylie Oates (1844–1862), also in Company F, died in Mississippi. According to their brother Calvin Greer Oates, he was wounded at Iuka, where he later died. In 1862, nineteen-year-old John Oates Dickey, son of Samuel B. and Mary Oates Dickey, was killed, having enlisted in Company B sometime after July 15, 1861. Seventeen-year-old Thomas Whitesides, son of James S. and Catherine Whitesides, also became a victim of the war in 1862.[19]

On August 27, Capt. Peter W. Parker, who had gone off to war with Company B, was back at Pisgah, where he married Mattie D. McArthur. He had served as captain of Company B, 2d Arkansas Cavalry, until the reorganization of his regiment at Corinth. Being over age, he resigned and came home, and later that year organized the Old Men's Company under General Hindman. He later returned to regular service in Sherman's battalion as a private and served in that company for the rest of the war. After the reorganization, the only Pisgah men in the noncommissioned officer ranks were James Q. Falls, second corporal, and Hiel F. Hughey, third corporal.[20]

By the summer of 1862, Union forces were on their way to gaining control of much of Arkansas. In May, Arkansas Unionists were encouraged by the arrival of General Curtis at Batesville, and Union units had been formed in some of the northern counties. On June 6 Memphis was captured, and Union forces now controlled the Mississippi River from St. Louis to Vicksburg. Later that month Union forces took possession of Helena. On September 22, President Lincoln issued the preliminary Emancipation Proclamation, which declared that slaves in the rebellious states would be free on or after January 1, 1863. In early January 1863, Gen. Thomas J. Churchill surrendered Arkansas Post to the Union army.

Despite, or because of, the Union advances in Arkansas, Pisgah men continued to volunteer for Confederate service. Andrew Kerr Henry, fifty years old, enlisted in the Confederate cavalry and served in a number of engagements. His son Silas Alexander Henry had gone into service with Ben T. Embry's Company B in 1861. Robert B. Whitesides also left his wife on his Galla Creek farm and enlisted, serving until the end of hostilities.[21]

Meanwhile, Company B was engaged in the Kentucky Campaign under Gen. Kirby Smith. They fought at Richmond, Kentucky, on August 30 and at Perryville on October 8. From December 31, 1862, to January 2, 1863, they fought at Murfreesboro, Tennessee, where a number were wounded: William Beck, John T. Falls Sr., John M. Ferguson, Hiel F. Hughey, Lorenzen D. Love, and Calvin Grier Oates. Falls was also captured.[22] Among these casualties were two who had been captured at Pea Ridge.

In August 1863, Federal troops began action that would place the Arkansas River Valley nominally in Federal hands. On September 7, troops moving from the east engaged the Confederates in a skirmish at Ashley's Mill and on September 10 occupied Little Rock. Meanwhile, in western Arkansas, on September 1, Federal troops reoccupied Fort Smith and began operations below that point on the river, bringing the war closer than it had come to Pisgah. On September 9, there were skirmishes at Dardanelle, which was occupied the following day after another skirmish. On October 28 and November 8 there were skirmishes at Clarksville, and on October 29 at Ozark. With these actions in the summer and fall of 1863, Confederate forces were forced south of the river, where they would remain until the end of the war.

In early 1864, Union forces backed the reorganization of state government. Governor Flanagin had retreated from Little Rock with the Confederate forces and moved the seat of Arkansas government to Washington in Hempstead County. In January 1864, delegates from twenty-four counties met at Little Rock, adopted a constitution, and installed Isaac Murphy as provisional governor. On April 18, the Union army supervised elections in counties with Unionist support. Isaac Murphy was elected governor, while the Confederate government of the state continued to function at Washington.

As soon as they had gained some degree of control of the Arkansas River Valley in 1863, Federal forces began recruiting local men for Union service. Crow Mountain, north and east of the Pisgah community, was located in Gum Log Township, which had considerable Union support. It supplied a number of men for the 2d Arkansas Infantry and the 3d Arkansas Cavalry. The former saw action at Prairie de Ann and Jenkins' Ferry and later at those places and at Marks' Mill. The Pisgah community also supplied troops for these units, including John Hughey and John Bradley with the 3d Arkansas Cavalry and Melvin Robertus Bradley, who died while serving with the 2d Arkansas Infantry. In the spring of 1864, the 3d Arkansas Cavalry under Col. A. H. Ryan was ordered to Lewisburg, where the unit remained until the end of the war. The 2d Arkansas Infantry under Col. Marshal L. Stephenson was stationed at Clarksville, where they, too, remained until war's end.[23] Pope County, and particularly communities in the valley like Pisgah, lay between these units and bore the brunt of many of their forays.

These units began engaging Confederates on a small scale. Though no major engagements took place, the combination of their foraging expeditions and the guerrilla warfare throughout the remainder of the war took a heavy toll in Pope County and surrounding regions. Skirmishes took place at Dardanelle on May 10 and May 15 through 19, at Norristown on May 19, and at Lewisburg on June 10, 1864. Scouting expeditions went out from Lewisburg in June, July, and August into Pope and Yell counties, and there were skirmishes in Yell County and at Dardanelle. In September, there were operations near Lewisburg and scouting expeditions to Norristown, Russellville, Fort Smith, and Strahan Landing. Skirmishes and scouting expeditions continued in the region through the winter and to the early spring of 1865.

While these events were transpiring near their homes, the Pisgah men who belonged to Company B were seeing major action in the east. In 1864, they fought at Jackson, Mississippi, on May 4; at Chickamauga, Tennessee, September 19 and 20; and in the Atlanta Campaign, May 8 through September 2 as part of Stuart's Company, Walthall's Division of Reynold's

Brigade. Then on November 30, they fought at Franklin, Tennessee, and December 15 and 16 at Nashville, and were part of the rearguard action in the retreat from Nashville to Florence, Alabama, December 17 through 19. By the following spring, when the war was winding down, they were in North Carolina, fighting at Bentonville on March 19 through 21. They were among the units surrendered to Gen. William T. Sherman at Greensboro on April 16, 1865.[24]

Company B had seen service through the war, from start to finish, as parts of the 2d Arkansas Mounted Rifles, 4th Arkansas Infantry, 9th Arkansas Infantry, and 25th Arkansas Infantry. Those on the surrender list were Silas Henry, B. H. Allen, Charles F. Clark, Robert H. Cleveland, Caleb Davis, James Q. Falls, Thomas L. Falls, Henry Hill, James H. Henry, James A. Oates, Thomas M. Oates, and J. E. Wilson. Of those, only eight had been among the original members of the company: Clark, Cleveland, James and Thomas Falls, Silas and James Henry, Henry Hill, and Thomas Oates. Silas Henry, a second lieutenant by then, was the only original officer.[25]

It is difficult to say that one Pisgah family suffered any more than another as a result of the war, but the agonies of some families were monumental. In April 1863, Elizabeth Neely McElwee (1797–1863) died and was buried at Pisgah. She and her husband, William, who had been senior immigrants of the early 1850s, had been touched deeply by the war. Their son William had been killed, leaving a wife and a young daughter. Their son-in-law, Joseph D. Oates, died in Mississippi, leaving a wife and two young boys. Daughters Melissa and Elizabeth Z. had husbands in the war. Elizabeth's husband, Dr. Alexander W. Henry, served as a doctor in the Confederate service. In 1864 he contracted malaria and died in service.[26] The McElwees also had grandsons Thomas B. and James McElwee in service.

Alexander and Mary Oates Bell sent six sons to the Confederate army. Franklin Robertus probably served throughout the war. John apparently enlisted early and served in Tennessee, Mississippi, and Georgia. At Moore's Mill near Atlanta he received a serious wound. Upon recovery, he was sent on furlough to the home of relatives in North Carolina to convalesce, but weakened by his wounds, he took typhoid and died in the winter of 1864–65. William served during most, if not all, of the war. He enlisted as a member of Company F, 1st Arkansas Cavalry and was among those who surrendered at the fall of Vicksburg. He was sent to Rock Island, Illinois, as a prisoner of war and spent some time there. Warren Bell served most, if not all, of the war in southern Arkansas, Louisiana, and Texas. Thomas Bell probably served no more than two years. He was a member of Company I, 1st Arkansas Battalion, and saw action at Mark's Mill and Jenkins' Ferry. Finally, Ewart Bell, the youngest, went into service in late 1864 and saw limited services with Company F, 22d Arkansas.[27]

Other families felt the horrors of war for another reason: divided loyalties in the conflict. A good example is the Hughey family. John (1843–?), third child of Henry (1812–1893) and Rebekah (Rebecca?) Hughey (1820–1885), enlisted in the Union army at Galley Rock on November 8, 1863, and was mustered into service two days later at Little Rock as a private in Company A, 3d Regiment, Arkansas Volunteer Cavalry. The first born of the Hughey children was Hiel F., who had intended to become a Presbyterian minister, which was no surprise in a family of devout Christians, apparently of the Seceder tradition and perhaps of the Convenanter. Like his ancestors, young Heil was attracted to the Psalms, memorized them, and could recite from memory all one hundred and fifty. According to family tradition, those Hugheys who left Tennessee and went to Arkansas were opposed to slavery. But twenty-three-year-old Hiel enlisted in Company B of the Arkansas Mounted Rifles sometime after July 15, 1861. His hopes to be a minister were cut short. He died in the war on November 22, 1863.[28]

Still other families suffered as a result of conflicts of conscience that put them at odds with the attitudes that prevailed in the Pisgah community. Hiram Patrick, cousin of the Reverend John Patrick and son-in-law of Cyrus Ewing, was conscripted on the Confederate side as was his brother-in-law Winter Ewing. Hiram served fourteen months during the first part of the war. He was in the battle of Helena, but he threw away his rifle to avoid killing anyone. His father-in-law got Hiram and Winter out of the army.[29] Another man of courage, a member of the session of Pisgah Church, who suffered for his convictions was Hugh Taylor (1808–?). Taylor had migrated from Lincoln County, Tennessee, in 1853 and found a place in the Pisgah community. He was a quiet man and highly respected. A justice of the peace, he signed many of the legal documents for members of the community, which recognized his Christian character and integrity by electing him a ruling elder at Pisgah in 1859. His son-in-law, William McElwee, had volunteered in 1861 with the Arkansas Mounted Rifles and had died shortly thereafter, leaving his wife, Mary, and small daughter. Yet Taylor was against secession. Since many of the Pisgah-Bethany people were so strong for the Confederate cause, community pressure was probably strong and patriotism linked to support of the Confederacy. We do not know how Hugh Taylor's friends tolerated his position, but we imagine there were great strains on his relationships. In March 1864, he sold his land, apparently in preparation for leaving Pope County. Years later, Taylor's son-in-law wrote that he was "a very strong Union man and had to leave things and go back North to keep from being killed by outlaws. He was a magistrate and a very quiet law abiding man."[30] Where Hugh Taylor and his family went in the north is not known.

By the time Taylor left Pisgah, the economic and political life of the community was devastated. A day book kept in 1861 and 1862 by Silas R. Parker, the merchant who ran Parker's Mill, gives a glimpse of the material culture of the community during the first year of the war. The gristmill, located on Galley Creek on the military road about a mile and a half south of Pottsville, was a popular place for buying supplies and having corn and wheat ground. Among Parker's customers were members of the Bell, Bigham, Dickey, Falls, Faulkner, Ferguson, Harbison, Hay, Henry, Hill, Hoffman, Kerr, Kirkpatrick, Love, McArthur, McElwee, Oates, Parker, Patrick, Quinn, Wells, and Whitesides families. Parker's ledger shows that in the early weeks after secession, he was dealing in fine clothes and accessories: shirts, vests, handkerchiefs, ties, pants, gloves, coats, shoes, and boots for men and coats, hose, and gloves for women. Items such as thimbles, thread, cloth, tobacco, molasses, and sugar were readily available. Patent medicines as well as medicinal supplies such as quinine, castor oil, laudanum, liniment, epsom salts, peppermint, paregoric, and fine whiskey were available to local physicians and others. By September of 1861, goods were still available, but there is evidence that money was devalued, for Parker was apparently cashing Confederate bonds at less than face value.[31] This was only one sign of a weakening economic system.

In addition, the community faced the problem of protecting itself in the absence of so many of its able-bodied men. At first, fear of community strife was directed toward the slaves. After secession, the Secession Convention acted as a provisional government for the state. On May 30,

1861, it directed the county courts to appoint Home Guards of Minute Men, consisting of at least ten men to serve for three months in each township. Their duties were to disarm all slaves and to prevent their meeting in "unusual numbers," and to keep them in "proper subjection." The Home Guards organized in Pope County on August 3, with Pisgah men in the ranks from both Galley Rock and Illinois townships. In Galley Rock, James Quinn was second lieutenant, and in the ranks were William B. Dickey, William Oates, and A. B. Taylor. In Illinois, William M. Galloway, Peter Hoffman, Thomas Oates, Robert Quinn, and Hugh Taylor were listed in the ranks.[32] In time, Pisgah would find that the danger came not from the slaves but from others in the county. During the next few years, outlawry and domestic terrorism further weakened the community. By war's end, Pisgah was devastated economically and rent by factionalism and political strife from which it would not fully recover.

# ❦ Chapter 7 ❦

# The Pisgah Home Front in War and Reconstruction

With the arrival of Union forces in the county in 1863, the Pisgah community began to deteriorate rapidly. Some with strong Confederate sympathies immediately left their homes to seek refuge elsewhere. One was Darling Love, who had migrated to Pope County from North Carolina in 1838, settling first on the military road east of Russellville and in 1853 moving to Holla Bend. When Federal troops arrived, he and his youngest son, Ransom D. Love, left their farm in early September 1863 and took refuge in Ellis County, Texas. Though underaged, the younger Love slipped away from home the following April and joined the 35th Texas Cavalry and saw his first combat at Pleasant Hills, Louisiana. Also fleeing the Federals, Sallie Parker Falls, wife of John Franklin Falls and sister to Capt. P. W. Parker, sought refuge in Sevier County, where she died.[1] Those who remained at Pisgah faced two years of outlawry and military occupation, and after the war, along with returning refugees and soldiers, faced additional civil strife, martial law, poverty, and lingering enmity that lasted for years.

With most of the able-bodied men in service, those left behind—old men, women, and children—fell prey to guerrilla bands that waged their own personal war in the Arkansas River Valley and account for the numerous skirmishes that occurred in the region. Some bands had ostensible links with one side or the other. Those allied with the Confederacy were called bushwhackers by Union sympathizers, and those with Union ties were called jayhawkers by the southerners. Some groups had a soldier in charge, but for the most part they were an undisciplined lot who hid out in the hills and conducted their raids on the defenseless communities. Some groups belonged to neither side but attacked both, committing acts of murder, arson, and robbery.[2] They swept down on defenseless women and children, pilfering and robbing of clothes, rustling cattle, emptying corn bins, taking whatever they wanted.

The Pisgah farms, prosperous at the start of the war and located in one of the county's most fertile sections, became prime targets for such villains. Ruffians called at the Sinclair home seeking gold. They refused to believe there was no more gold hidden by the Sinclairs. The bandits heated a fire shovel red hot and threatened to burn the soles of old Gregory Sinclair's feet. When Nancy McElwee Oates refused to tell where their gold was, they carried out their threat.[3]

After a time, lawlessness in the valley began to drive families out. Cyrus Ewing, a Union sympathizer, took his family to Mitchell, Indiana, in August 1864. He explained why he left the Cove: "I stood my ground and fought the rebels till they robbed us of nearly everything we had. Money, horses, bedding, clothing. They took from Eliza and Georgia shawls, stockings, caps, left us nearly destitute." Whether he meant by "rebels" the Confederate army, bushwhackers, or just outlaws is uncertain. He had been holding one hundred dollars of his sister's money since the war broke out, afraid to send it through the mails. He used it to escape: "It had to be spent to get us out of the Jaws of the Devil." Ewing's son-in-law, Hiram Patrick, had worked for the Federals in Little Rock after Ewing got him out the Confederate army and, according to Ewing, "got his family" out and went with some friends to Springfield, Illinois.[4] Among them was perhaps Henry Vandever from Illinois, who was living in John Patrick's home in 1860, along with William and Sarah Patrick Peeler. On the Confederate side, the farm of Andrew Nael Falls on the military road was robbed again and again. The family devised a hiding place under the smokehouse to take refuge from the looters. Finally, they were pillaged and harassed so often that they could stand it no longer. The Falls family along with their daughter Ann and her husband, James Quinn, moved to Wood County, Texas, where Quinn died.[5]

Pisgah residents had to contend with not only bushwhackers and jay-hawkers but regular army units as well. When foraging parties invaded the community, civilians were forced to give up what they could not successfully hide. In 1864 the 3d U.S. Cavalry occupied Lewisburg, and the 2d Arkansas Infantry was stationed at Clarksville, where they remained until the end of the war.[6] Armies had to be fed and clothed, and the Federal troops were no exception. Jane Henry Ferguson saw Federal troops come to the Andrew Kerr Henry farm and carry off twenty-five wagon-loads of provisions at one time. Melissa McElwee Oates, whose husband, Thomas, was serving in the Confederate army, was left with at least five children to feed. She buried provisions to keep the bushwhackers from finding them, but she also faced the visits of Federal troops seeking supplies. One day, when they visited her farm, an officer found a bolt of woolen cloth which Melissa had made, took it, and tied it on his saddle. As he was about to ride away, Melissa came up to the horse, untied the bolt, and told the officer, "I made this for clothes for my children." Reports coming through the Wade Oates family say that the officer did not say a word and let her keep the cloth without controversy. Melissa's resourcefulness was reflected in other actions. When she received word that her husband had been shot in the neck and was recuperating after the battle at Jenkins' Ferry in April 1864, she hitched an oxen team to a wagon, loaded her children, and went to Jenkins' Ferry, where she became Thomas's nurse. She and the children stayed until he was on his way to recovery.[7]

The Gregory Sinclair farm sat on the strategic military road and suffered incursions by both the military and looters. One day, a squad of Federal troops confiscated all their horses and mules, told their slaves that they were free, and ordered a young slave named Jim to mount one of the mules and go with them. "Night riders were frequent visitors for the next eighteen months," wrote Molly Sinclair Falls. "In fact, we were robbed seven times. During the first few visits, they always found money but this soon gave out. At one time, sister Margaret and myself hid $500.00 gold in a glass jar. This was also a total loss to us as we presume that someone saw us bury the money, then soon unearthed it." Their brother was once slightly wounded by robbers but managed to make his escape. "No one except those who experienced it," Molly Falls wrote, "can fully appreciate just what we underwent during the closing days of the Civil War."[8]

The actions of Melissa Oates, Molly Falls, and others demonstrate that survival of the community depended much upon the resourcefulness of the women. They became partisans and message carriers. One Sinclair family story tells of a group of Confederate soldiers who became separated from their company and hid out in the bluffs of Crow Mountain to act as a Home Guard. It was the task of the Confederate daughters to carry food to them. They showed the girls how to conceal supplies under their hoop skirts by suspending them from strings tied around their waists and showed them how to walk so that they would make no noise in the leaves and twigs on the ground. "Frequently," says one Sinclair descendant, "the officers and men of the occupying forces made themselves at home in the Sinclair home on the Wire Road. While they were in the dining room eating, Margaret, aged 13 or 14, would filch ammunition from their packs and send it to the Confederate soldiers."[9]

As the war continued, men in the military service, both Confederate and Union, worried about the families they had left behind. In December 1864, Darling Love, who was in the army with several of his sons, made his way through Federal lines to his home in Holla Bend and took his wife with him back to Ellis County, Texas, where she remained until the war was over.[10] That same year, Dr. Alexander W. Henry, a physician in the Confederate army, wrote his "Dear Wife, Mother & Sisters" from Hempstead County: "I want to see you very much, I don't know when I will, however, I think perhaps you would do well to try to get out and come south, but you will hear more from me before long. Kiss the babes for me, give my love to all friends." This was not the first time Henry had been separated from his family. In 1857 he had gone into the residency in the medical department of Nashville University for training. Lonesome, he asked his wife and mother to write him "every thing, for any will interest me that comes from home."[11]

Union soldiers from the community also worried about their families left behind. A good example was John M. Bradley, who left his wife and nine children on his farm in the Cove and enlisted in Company A, 3d Regiment, Arkansas "C" Volunteers, on October 18, 1863. On February 12, 1865, he wrote his wife, Sarah, from Lewisburg, where he expected to be at least until spring. If he did not get to come home then, he wanted Sarah to come and see him. Bradley had considered sending his family north. He had talked about it with a friend who had been there, but the friend advised him, he said, "to keep my family here if they could live at all. So I am satisfied for the present." But he was worried about his teenaged son Albert. It was a dangerous age for a boy to be in the Cove. "I do not think he will be safe at home," Bradley wrote, and he contemplated trying to get his son a job at Lewisburg for the summer. Bradley worked out a proverb for his children that read:

Children one and
all obey your
mother and doo that
is right.[12]

Bradley was concerned about his family's supply of food. "I heard that thain taken nearly all your corn and oats that is nothing more than I expected," he wrote. The crops had apparently been confiscated by Federal troops, for he said, "If you have a recit For your corn and oats send it Down the first chance," apparently so that he might get reimbursement. Bradley worried if they had enough to do them for the summer. He hoped Sarah had been able to get the cotton ginned, but did not want her to send it to Lewisburg because the roads were so bad that he did not know if it would get there. He would let her know when to send it to Little Rock, for there was "such a fuss Bout coton and I canot ship it to the Rock at present," even if he had it at Lewisburg. John was also concerned about the approaching planting season. He urged Sarah to buy "Widow James Mayes Blind mare if you have to pay Forty Dollars. She is a good mare and gentle and the best chance that I noe of For to make a crop." He wanted Sarah to plant plenty of potatoes. If some land had to be left uncultivated, she should plant the good land, and let the other lie fallow.[13] There was one bright note in Bradley's letter: there was talk of a "big excitement" of peace, expected in the spring.

The bloody conflict in which Pisgah men had been engaged was, in fact, winding down, but the Pisgah community would continue to sacrifice its members to the end of the war and beyond. John Franklin Falls, son of Andrew Nael and Margaret Quinn Falls, was selling merchandise at Parker's Mill and Store when the war started and volunteered for Confederate service in 1862. His wife, Sallie Parker Falls, had gone to Sevier County in 1863, where she had died a refugee. During Gen. Sterling Price's last raid into Missouri, John Franklin Falls was wounded and taken prisoner and died while a prisoner.[14] The Henry M. Hughey family, who had already lost one son in the Confederate army, lost a second son, Isaac, only eleven days before Lee's surrender. Twenty-year-old Isaac was at home on furlough from the Union army. On March 29, 1865, he "was shot and killed on the porch of Mrs. Eliza Reed's farm home west of Russellville by Confederate soldiers or sympathizers. It is said the bloodstains could be seen for years on the spot. Isaac was buried in Pisgah Cemetery."[15]

On April 9, Gen. Robert E. Lee surrendered to Gen. U. S. Grant at Appomattox, effectively bringing the war to an end. The price to the Pisgah community had been high. Pisgah had sent nearly sixty men to the war, fifteen of whom had been lost. Though the war officially ended with the surrender, Pisgah would give up one more.

On April 21, almost three weeks after the death of Isaac Hughey, the body of Franklin Robertus Bell was discovered in a creek. Bell, who apparently had been a guerrilla fighter in the area, has been described as "a hard riding, daring cavalry soldier and after the occupation of this area by Federal troops and when local residents were at the mercy of the Bushwhackers, his name became a holy terror. There is little doubt that services of this type cost him his life. At least the facts are that he surrendered as a prisoner of war at Louisburg [Lewisburg], now South Morrilton, at the conclusion of the war." Stories vary regarding the details of the killing, but all agree that he was apparently shot by bushwhackers when he stopped at the creek to get a drink, either on his way to Lewisburg or on his way home from there.[16]

Peace did not bring an end to the bitterness and animosities engendered by the long years of war. One writer has said, "Men deserted both armies to return home to get revenge for a wrong done to their families. Thus before the Civil War ended, a war of vengeance was begun. It was an undeclared war with no formal start or finish. Emotions were high and men lost their reason. Hearsay evidence was cause enough to shoot." He continues, "Discharged soldiers returned home to be greeted by sorrow and financial disaster throughout the former Confederate states. In the Valley, the ex-soldier returned to all this and to a new war. It was a different kind of war—fought with such bitterness that all who experienced it always remembered."[17] The Pisgah community, too, would suffer from a lingering bitterness. The terrible toll that the war had taken on the people and the farms of the community left a blighted legacy to the men returning from war. They faced the herculean task of rebuilding the community, and they would do it valiantly.

When the Confederate army west of the Mississippi formally surrendered on May 26, 1865, Pope County, like much of the south, was an economic disaster. The Pisgah community, because of its location in a fertile region, had seen its prosperous farmers reduced to subsistence and many of its people scattered as soldiers and refugees. Those who had managed to survive the war at home, despite the army foragers on both sides and the bushwhackers and jayhawkers, put in a crop in the spring of 1865 as best they could with what farming equipment and animals were left to them. Meanwhile, refugees and soldiers began to find their way back home from far and near, and the community began to try to put itself together again.

The pro-Confederate families of the region, especially those who had owned slaves and had become refugees in southern Arkansas or Texas, began to return to the region even before the surrender of the Confederate army under Gen. E. Kirby Smith was completed. Though the Arkansas River Valley was still torn by violence in the spring of 1865, many braved the dangers in an attempt to get back home to plant a corn crop before the season was too far advanced.[18]

A good example is the Andrew Nael Falls family, who had taken refuge in Wood County, Texas, during the last two years of the war. On their return, the Falls family brought their former slaves, now freed. Falls's loss of property in slaves was not as considerable as that of others, for he had only three in 1860. But the desolation of his farm and his loss of crops, livestock, and goods were great. In 1860, Falls owned 65 improved and 335 unimproved acres valued at $5,000. He produced that year 86 bushels of wheat, 700 of corn, 100 pounds of tobacco, and seven bales of cotton. He also had sixteen head of cattle, fifteen sheep, and one hundred swine, as well as a horse and his work mules.[19] He returned to Pope County in 1865 with little else but his land.

Falls's situation was typical. One ex-Confederate soldier wrote, "The returned refugees found the country naked, except a spot here and there where neighborhoods had been of one mind and had been faithful to each other; but they found their farms in a bad condition for raising a hurried crop. However, all who returned before the last of June, by hard labor and hard living, succeeded in raising a fair crop of late corn."[20] The soldiers, who began to straggle back to their homes, faced similar situations. Those lucky enough to have families at home to begin a crop were far ahead of those who had to depend on themselves.

Some, like James Quinn Falls, were far from home when the war ended. He had furnished his own horse and rifle and was mustered into the 2d Arkansas Mounted Rifles at Bentonville in 1861, one of an estimated thirty Pisgah men who joined that unit under Ben T. Embry. The unit had fought at Wilson's Creek and at Pea Ridge. In the summer of 1863, Falls was still with the unit when it mustered into the 25th Consolidated Rifles, with which he fought through Tennessee, Georgia, South Carolina, and North Carolina. He was on the surrender list for Company B, one of only eight of the company's original members to fight with it through the entire war. At Hendersonville, he was paroled as a prisoner of war two weeks after Lee's surrender at Appomattox. Though he had escaped the war without a wound, as Falls made his way back home, he was shot in the hand by a bushwhacker in Tennessee.[21]

Another man paroled far from home at about the same time was Silas Henry. At nineteen, he had joined what would become Company B at Galla Rock. Like Falls, he fought through the war with Company B and was a veteran of a number of battles. He was wounded twice, slightly at Chickamauga and seriously at Franklin, Tennessee. At war's end, he surrendered under Joseph E. Johnson at Greensboro, North Carolina, on May 14, 1865, one of only eight of the original members and the only officer of Company B. Henry was kept in a military prison hospital at Knoxville from May 22 to June 14, suffering from typhoid fever, and was released from there. He reached home on July 5 and went back to farming.[22] It is uncertain how or when others of Company B, including James A. Oates, Thomas Oates, Thomas Falls, and James Henry, made their way back to Pisgah.

Others were not as far from home, but were nevertheless slow in returning. William M. Peeler had enlisted in Company B and fought with them at Pea Ridge but became ill and could not go with the unit east of the Mississippi in 1862. He recovered and joined Company H, 22d Arkansas Regiment and served at Helena and Little Rock and in Louisiana, ultimately reaching the rank of captain. He surrendered at Marshall, Texas, and reached Pope County on June 13. Peter W. Parker had ended his second stint in the army with a company of Sherman's Battalion, which disbanded on the Red River in Arkansas, "but on account of the unsettled state of affairs" in Pope County, he did not return home until August of 1865. Before the war, the Parkers had operated a store and gristmill as well as a plantation farmed by slaves, of which Silas R. Parker owned twenty-four.

He had 55 improved and 345 unimproved acres, on which he raised corn, tobacco in great quantities, and hogs in large numbers. Parker returned to find his father's store devastated and his farm very rundown. He went to work to build back his farm, and when his father, Silas, died in 1867, he took over the store and mill.[23] Still others, like John M. Bradley, who was in the Union army at Lewisburg, were near at hand and could make it home in plenty of time to help with the crops.[24]

In contrast, Calvin Grier Oates had left Pisgah in 1861 with Company B and was in the war four years. He was captured at Pea Ridge but somehow managed to rejoin his unit and was later captured again and spent fourteen months as a prisoner of war. After the war he went to Texas and did not return to Pisgah until October 1. There, he found his half sister Margaret Bigham and her daughter Nancy still at home and learned that his nineteen-year-old brother, Sam, had enlisted in the army and had been killed.[25] He settled down on the old homestead, repaired the farm, and reentered the church life of Pisgah, which he had joined in 1861.

Fortunately for the returning refugees and soldiers, Federal troops were stationed at Dardanelle. Said one Yell County Confederate veteran,

> They were a protection to the refugees, for this country had been very much divided during the last two years of the war between southern sympathizers, who had remained at home, and the families of Union sympathizers, who had also remained at home, the people of both parties had been most mercilessly robbed and maltreated by confederate bush-whackers on the one hand, and federal mountain-boomers on the other, so that both sides were in great need of the necessaries of life, and the feelings of hate and revenge ran high, and now that the confederates had laid down their arms, they were at the mercy of the mountain-boomers, who had it not been for the regular federal soldiers at Dardanelle, would have taken revenge upon the returning refugees, for what the confederate bush-whackers had done in the way of murder and robbery.[26]

He continued, "I would not reflect too severely upon the mountain-boomers and federal sympathizers of this country, for be it said to their credit, that thefts, robberies and murders ceased at once, as soon as the confederates of the army returned to their homes."[27] Still, a smoldering resentment persisted among those who had stayed, matched by resentment among the refugees. Many refugees were distressed by what they found upon their return, especially the pro-Union refugees who had farther to travel and who were much later in returning.

A good example was Cyrus Ewing. Ewing, who had fled from Bradley's Cove to Mitchell, Indiana, in 1864, left New Albany, Indiana, on a dark, stormy midnight in late October 1865 aboard the boat *Camelia*. The following morning Ewing discovered that a large box containing a folding leaf table, feather bed, blankets, bolsters, pillows, sheets, clothing, hats, books, and other items had been left on the wharf along with two windsor and two split-bottom chairs. Though Ewing wrote the boat owner trying to retrieve his property, it was never found. Thus the Ewings arrived at Norristown in November "with very little of anything" in the way of personal property, and "no horse, cow, hog, very little money." Planting season was months away and the next harvest even farther. Thus he joined the ranks of the destitute people of the region. He drew about sixty dollars from the Reverend John Patrick on a note he held in behalf of his sister Elizabeth Ewing for the land she had sold Patrick when he came to Pisgah as minister. Ewing needed the money to survive; he paid twelve dollars for pork, and bought corn at two dollars per bushel. He wrote his brother, "We have bought a very old mule to tend a crop on credit. The boys Winter and Hale are industrious, working hard to try to accumulate something again. Our dear son DeWitt we have had no account of since the Battle at Springfield, Missouri in Dec. 1862. We suppose he was killed."[28]

A month after Cyrus Ewing returned, his son-in-law Hiram Patrick and family returned from Illinois. Paper was scarce, but Ewing found a scrap to write his brother about Hiram and Erie Patrick's destitution, how they were "scuffing to make a living." Like his cousin John Patrick, Hiram owed Elizabeth Ewing money for land he had bought before the war, but they could not possibly pay her anything until the next crop was made. That was months away, in the fall of 1866. Much turned on that next crop. "We are dependent on the North for something to eat," Cyrus Ewing wrote in April of that year. "The prospect for wheat is tolerable good at present. When harvest comes we think we will have bread a plenty. As the old saying goes: Live Horse, and you shall have fodder after a while."[29]

During the next several months, Ewing tried in vain to collect the money that was owed his sister, who was also in a difficult economic condition in Kentucky. He defended Hiram Patrick in his debt. He was at "home working hard to accumulate something again," but by the summer of 1866, it appeared that he would not be able for another year to pay Elizabeth anything of the three hundred dollars he still owed her. Ewing was right, for after the fall crop came in 1866, there was still no money to spare, and Hiram could not pay. To Ewing, however, the Reverend John Patrick was another matter. Ewing vowed to "compell" him to pay the estimated two hundred dollars he still owed Elizabeth.[30]

Ewing's attitude toward Patrick reflected the bitterness that gripped him as a result of the war. "It will not be worth my time," he wrote his sister, "to write a long account of our tribulations in this cursed war. Suffice to say it has taken all we had except our home." But that was not all. Word came in the summer of 1866 that his son DeWitt was, in fact, dead. Staunch in his Unionist beliefs, he had written his brother, "Let your watch word be Remember Abraham Lincoln." Destitute, unable to collect the debts owed his family, he began to focus his bitterness toward the rebels on Patrick, of whom he said, "He was a bad rebel in the war and it has worsted him a good deal. I am ready to say 'Amen' to all the suffering of all the Rebels."[31]

Ewing's statement reflects the strong animosities that existed not only in the extended Pisgah community but throughout Pope County. For two years following the war, the county had episodes of relative quiet punctuated by political violence and assassination of county officials. The unresolved conflicts between former Confederates and Unionists underpinned the political violence. The first sheriff following the war was Dodson Napier, a former Union captain. He and his deputy named Parks were shot and killed on a public road near Dover on October 25, 1865. In 1866, the first postwar clerk, William Stout, was killed at Dover, and William Hickox, also a former Federal officer, became clerk. W. Morris Williams from Hector, who was appointed sheriff to replace Napier, was killed while plowing his field in August 1866. E. W. Dodson, another former U.S. captain, was appointed in his place.[32] One writer from Dover called for calm after Williams's murder, saying it was "calculated to create—(especially among a people already in discord in memory of the late struggle)—a disturbance that would prove disastrous and terrific in our now peaceful community." Another wrote that the event was blown out of proportion by the radical Republican party: "They must need keep alive a bitter sectional and partisan spirit in the North, in order to retain their hold on the political power of the country."[33] The political difficulties continued until two companies of U.S. regulars under the command of Major Mulligan were sent to Dover in the spring of 1867. During the following eighteen months, while the troops were there, relative peace reigned.[34]

The presence of troops may have brought a temporary political order, but the personal animosities continued to seethe under the surface. Shortly before the troops arrived in 1867, Cyrus Ewing wrote, "Rebels are overbearing. They say they are not whipped. They take a great deal of pride in wearing the Rebel Gray, both male and female. They are often told by the Blue Coats the blue means true and gray means secede and want to get back in the Union again with their negroes. It makes them gnash their teeth. Union leagues are forming in every county to protect the country from danger of the Rebels. The poor negroes are very much imposed on by the Rebels. They have worked hard. Many of them sold their cotton crop for money and are robbed of it in a few hours afterwards. Instances of this kind in our county. One poor old negro suffered death before he would give up his money."[35]

Economic recovery was slow. The Ewing family letters indicate that the people lived in dire circumstances through the end of 1867. "Times are hard and money scarce" became Cyrus Ewing's common complaint.[36] Monroe Oates, who came to Pisgah as its pastor in early 1868, says of the Pisgah farmers, "The soldiers just returning home without stock, or farming utensils, without money, were compelled to get their supplies on credit. Consequently most of them were involved in debt. . . . There was such a state of feeling between the soldiers who had fought on different sides in the war that pistols were carried by many when going to town or traveling in the country. In many houses pistols could be seen hanging on the bed posts. This manifested a feeling of insecurity."[37]

The war had also ravaged the Pisgah Church, though at first, throughout the state, the Associate Reformed Presbyterian Church had maintained a semblance of normalcy in its activities. From Saline Township west of Monticello went a petition to the Arkansas Presbytery to organize a church. The petition was granted on August 31, 1861, and the Reverend J. M. Brown was appointed to carry out the order, which he did on the third Sabbath in October.[38] When the general assembly of the Presbyterian Church in the Confederate States met to organize in Augusta, Georgia, in December that year, the Associate Reformed Synod of the South considered a merger because of the common sympathy it held for the Confederacy and sent the Reverend Henry Quigg to the meeting. Both sides agreed that they were bound by the same faith, having the same symbols, and the Presbyterians of the South offered to print the entire Psalter in a new proposed hymnbook to accommodate the Associate Reformed Church. The new Southern Presbyterian Church was by far the closest relative of the Associate Reformed Presbyterian Church in the South. Both were ardent in their views on the inspiration of scripture, both adhered to the Westminster Confession of Faith, both were firm in their support of an educated ministry, and many Southern Presbyterians liked to sing Psalms. The merger did not take place, but most of the ministers and some of the churches nevertheless went into the Presbyterian Church.[39] Thus the war took a greater toll on the Associate Reformed Church than on the Southern Presbyterian Church because of its smallness, its scattered churches, and the weakened condition that resulted from its loss of members to its larger relative.

Since its founding in 1853, Pisgah Church had developed as one of the strongest churches in Pope County and one of the outstanding rural churches in the Arkansas River Valley. This was due largely to the constant migration of large, substantial families from North Carolina, South Carolina, and Tennessee. "But when the church was in the zenith of its prosperity," Monroe Oates writes, "many of its members became disorderly. Saloons were common and dram-drinking was practiced by many of its members. It is painful to read the church records from 1860 to 1862. Intemperance and strife prevailed to a lamentable extent. At one meeting of the Session as many as six cases of intemperance were under consideration."[40] Church discipline was required and frequently occurred.[41]

Perhaps in response to these unsettling developments, "it was thought necessary to increase the Eldership in early 1862." R. H. Dickey, T. M. Oates, Thomas Oates, and Samuel B. Dickey were chosen new members and ordained to the eldership by the Reverend John Patrick on February 12.[42] Samuel Dickey had been a member of Pisgah Church in North Carolina "during the pastorate of the distinguished minister, Dr. R. C. Grier." Dickey had married Mary McGill Oates, settled near Kings Mountain, and transferred his membership to Nebo before migrating to the west. Upon Dickey's death, Monroe Oates said that "he was known throughout the Pisgah community as quiet, retired and unobtrusive in his manners, diffident in expressing his opinions on disputed subjects. He was a man of peace. 'An Israelite in whom there was no guile.' Kept well the door of his lips, and would not tolerate in his family the repeating of a slanderous report on a neighbor. A strict observer of the Sabbath and a firm yet mild disciplinarian in family government."[43] Thomas Oates (1821–1904), the third son of John IV and Elizabeth McClure Oates, was born in Gaston County, North Carolina, and married Melissa G. McElwee, the daughter of William and Elizabeth Neely McElwee of York County, South Carolina. The couple settled in Gaston County and migrated to Pope County in 1853. His half brother, Calvin Grier Oates, said of him, "His interest in the church was one of his distinguishing characteristics."[44]

The year these men were elected elders was a difficult one for the church. Monroe Oates writes, "In 1862, division, alienation and animosity sprang up which paralized the energies of the church and separated intimate and dear friends."[45] Elsewhere, Oates writes practically the same thing: "Peace and harmony of the church was greatly disturbed. Animosity, division and strife prevailed to such an extent as to paralyze the energies of the Church."[46]

At this crucial time, the church lost its minister. Twenty-five-year-old David James Harvey Kerr, who had been sent as a minister in 1860, was well received at Pisgah, and the synod sent him back in 1861. On March 5, 1862, he married Nancy R. Oates, the daughter of the late John F. Oates V and Eliza McElwee Oates. With the marriage, Kerr acquired a host of family connections among the Pisgah community at large. Two months later he volunteered for Confederate service and requested the Reverend John Patrick to supply his place. Kerr returned in June and remained at Pisgah through the summer, but how long he remained is uncertain.[47] Oates indicates that the Reverend John Patrick tried to bring order in the church, but the difficulties cut to the heart of church governance. "We find the rod of discipline in the hand of Father Patrick and part of the Session," he wrote. "For it appears that some members of the Session were disorderly."[48] The elders at the time, in addition to the four just elected, were Dr. Franklin Raymond, Alexander Dickey, Hugh Taylor, A. N. Falls, James Quinn, Thomas Franklin, and James McElwee. He does not say which members were disorderly, but he has given us a picture of "Pisgah in turmoil."

What, beyond the dram drinking, were the origins of the alienation and animosity that now rent the once-unified church community? Feelings ran high during the sectional debate leading to the war. It may be that that controversy infected the minds of the covered-wagon settlers and colored their thinking in 1861 and 1862. The church was further weakened by the exigencies of war. Pisgah was a patriarchal society. With an estimated more than fifty of its men and boys taken for military service, including two of the elders elected in 1862, the practice of religion in the homes had to have altered drastically.

But Oates's dating the controversy in 1862 suggests a more specific cause, which was aggravated by the war. He says, in reference to it, "There were likewise feelings engendered by the war, which were the cause of some going to other churches who naturally belong to the A. R. P. church. The subject of union between the A. R. church and the Presbyterian church had been discussed, and most of the ministers and part of the churches had gone into the Presbyterian church."[49] That the controversy erupted at Pisgah after the conference of the Southern Presbyterians in late 1861 and early 1862 is significant. Oates's language suggests that the controversy was somehow related to Pisgah's refusal to join the Presbyterian Church. Thus, he writes, "When Rev. J. S. Willbanks organized Mount Zion, two or three influential A. R. P. families who had become disaffected went into that organization. Some predicted that the A. R. P. church would go down. But a church loses no strength by the departure from her fold of dissatisfied, disaffected members, who will not work for her welfare, more especially if such oppose the enterprises of the church."[50]

The war also interrupted preaching at Pisgah. On May 9, 1863, the Reverend David Kerr, who had apparently not preached at Pisgah since 1862, was ordained by the Arkansas Presbytery, but "from that time until 1866 he was in Drew County, Arkansas, teaching school and supplying vacancies. In 1866 he connected himself with the Presbyterian Church in the United States."[51] Monroe Oates writes, "In the absence of records we suppose that the regular preaching of the Word was very much interrupted after the latter part of 1863 until the end of the war. As the women who remained at home had no means of going to church except walking."[52] Whatever services were conducted under the circumstances were conducted by Patrick, who was the stated supply at Pisgah from May 1863 until

December 1867.[53] Other churches in the state had similar experiences. The Prosperity Church community in Fulton County "was repeatedly overrun by the contending factions and impoverished by foraging parties during the turbulent period of civil strife from 1861–1865." As at Pisgah, "The neighborhood was overrun by both armies. The armies added to the hardships of the people by taking their horses, mules and provisions. More than once the home of the pastor of Prosperity, Reverend W. S. Moffatt, was ransacked and his life was in danger from jayhawkers and bushwhackers."[54]

The economy of the Pisgah community ultimately recovered. Oates says that the high price of agricultural products, especially cotton at twenty-five to thirty cents a pound helped the congregation "recover rapidly from their financial embarrassment."[55] Though they may have been relieved of their embarrassment, the community as a whole would not recover the prosperity it had enjoyed in the 1850s, and, because of geographical shifts in the population, the church itself would be moved to Potts Station in the 1880s after the railway came, though the congregation would remain, worshiping there and at Bethany. As for the people, their bitterness resulting from warfare, deprivation, and loss of life and property would last well into the twentieth century.

# ❧ Chapter 8 ❧

# Rebuilding Pisgah

At war's end, Pisgah Church was in need of a minister. The Reverend David Kerr had not returned, and John Patrick, who had served the church as best he could during the war years, was getting old, he was debt-ridden, and he was ill. Thus Pisgah petitioned for a minister. Not just any minister would do. Even though the whole countryside was lying desolate, they would have an "educated minister or they would wait till they could get one." Although there were poor educational advantages in rural Arkansas, and practically none in their neighborhood at war's end, the Pisgah congregation clung to their tradition: their minister must have gone to college and seminary to be educated according to their standards, or he was not to be considered. Under postwar circumstances, they were fortunate to find Monroe Oates, a member of one of the community's most prominent families. It would be his task to see his congregation through difficult economic times and to help them overcome political conflict and personal animosities in an attempt to rebuild the Pisgah church community.

More information is available about Monroe Oates's early life than about the lives of other ministers who were at Pisgah, partly because he was closer in years to the present, and family memories were passed to succeeding generations about him and his wife. He also left a paper trail largely preserved by the people of the Pottsville Associate Reformed Presbyterian Church. Monroe Oates was the son of John IV and Elizabeth McClure Oates, born on June 30, 1832, "under the shadow of Crowder's Mountain," where, as one who knew him said, "his youth was spent among scenes as fill the soul with hope and the mind with ambition." When his father and most of his family moved from North Carolina to Arkansas in 1851, Oates stayed with his brother John Franklin Oates V in York County, South Carolina, to attend school. His preparation for college was at Hickory Grove, South Carolina. In the fall of 1852 he entered the sophomore class at Erskine College, and he graduated in 1855. That fall, he entered Erskine Theological Seminary.[1]

One of Oates's classmates, William Hood, wrote of him:

> Mr. Oates was an amiable classmate and companion, always kind and obliging, and never out of temper. If the thing to be done had a right and a wrong side of it, you would certainly find him on the side where right lay. He lived in close accord with his own conscience in close harmony with the word of God. No other book, no other kind of work, no kind of amusement ever tempted him to neglect the daily reading of the Bible. This was the standard to which everything was referred.[2]

Oates finished Erskine Theological Seminary in 1858 and received license for the First Presbytery on September 7, 1858. He visited Arkansas in 1858 to see his family before entering his duties and preached in Pope, Drew, Hempstead, and Fulton counties. In February 1859, he went to Virginia Presbytery and labored most of the time at the New Lebanon Church, Monroe County, Virginia, now West Virginia.[3] It was there that he became acquainted with the family of James Finley and Patsy Moore Harper of Lexington, Virginia. Harper was a merchant, a man of substance, whose family had been among the founders of the Ebenezer Associate Reformed Church. Oates courted the Harpers' daughter, Amanda Susan, and they were married on September 6, 1860, by Dr. William M. McElwee, Ebenezer's pastor, who had been reared in the Bethany community in York County, South Carolina.[4]

The couple traveled south so that Oates could attend the meeting of the synod at Hopewell, Georgia. Although he had "labored with great acceptance" at the New Lebanon Church, and the congregation "petitioned for his return," the synod placed him in new fields. He was sent to Pleasant Grove Church, Decatur County, Georgia. There, he supplied that church as well as one in Florida from October 1860 to October 1861. While they were at Pleasant Grove, a daughter, Mattie McClure, was born to the couple on June 25, 1861. The synod directed him to spend the next year in the First and Virginia Presbyteries, but the war prevented him from reaching his appointments in Virginia. Thus he spent the year supplying Smyrna in York County, South Carolina, and Knob Creek, North Carolina. The First Presbytery ordained him in 1862 and installed him as pastor of Smyrna on November 5, 1863.[5]

During the pastorate at Smyrna, Oates volunteered for services in the Confederacy. He entered the military service in 1864, "when a call was made for the old men, the boys, and the preachers," and reported to Columbia, South Carolina, where he remained for some time. But according to a friend, "his company was never supplied with guns and could not make a very strong opposition to Sherman's march. For some reason Oates was sent home just the day before the federals bombarded Columbia and thus escaped a hard march to escape capture." He was honorably discharged,[6] and he returned to Smyrna to resume his ministry, remaining there until 1867 when Pisgah's congregation invited him to their church.

That year, the synod transferred Oates to the Arkansas Presbytery. By that time his family had grown, with Franklin born in 1863 and Elizabeth in 1866. With the children, Monroe and Amanda Oates traveled to Arkansas, arriving about the fourteenth or fifteenth of December.[7] The sad economic condition of the community is reflected in Oates's description of the home that awaited the family. "The dwelling houses at that time were unpretentious," he wrote. "There were only three frame houses in the congregation. The house in which I first lived was made of logs with boards nailed on the cracks for weather boarding and ceiling. It consisted of one room with no ceiling overhead. No stoves, no carpets, or bedroom sets were provided."[8] Oates began his work among the congregation in early January 1868 and was formally installed on the fifth Monday in August. Entering the work at Pisgah under reduced circumstances, he had much in common with his congregation, who were engaged in the struggle for economic recovery.

Monroe Oates clearly understood that the condition of the church directly related to the economic condition of the congregation. Though he says that the Pisgah farmers quickly recovered from their "financial embarrassment" because of the high price of agricultural products, particularly cotton, evidence indicates that they did not at first shift to cash-crop production and that general economic recovery was slow. One result of the war's devastation and neglect of farms had been a significant decline in the value of real property throughout the state.[9] As late as 1870, most Pisgah farmers reported both real and personal property below the levels they had reported in 1860. The total valuation of taxable property for some declined by 50 percent or more. Gregory Sinclair and Elizabeth E. Oates, who had land holdings in 1870 comparable to what they had in 1860, are good examples. In 1870, Sinclair's real property, valued at $3,000 in 1860, was valued at $2,400 in 1870, and his personal property at $6,071 and $1,831, respectively. In 1860, Oates reported $6,600 in real property, valued at $3,700 in 1870, and personal property of $9,400 and $1,147, respectively. The greater decline for Sinclair and Oates as for other Pisgah residents was in personal property. Much of the loss sustained in personal property by these two and others such as A. N. Falls resulted from the loss of their slaves.[10]

There were, however, exceptions to the rule. One was James Whitesides, whose total property valuation went from $2,040 in 1860 to $4,100 in 1870. Like others in his community, he suffered a loss in the value of his real property, dropping from $2,400 to $1,900. However, his gain came in personal property, which rose from $1,341 to $2,200 in 1870. Whitesides was not a slave owner, but neither were many in the community who materially were far worse off in 1870 than they had been before the war. Part of the explanation lies in the kind of farming Whitesides was engaged in. In 1870, the farming practices of Pisgah farmers in general looked little different from those of 1860. There were no work oxen, which had been replaced by horses and mules. Grain production, though generally less, was still mainly in corn and wheat. Hogs, though not kept in such numbers as in 1860, a few milk cows, and sheep, generally in larger flocks than in 1860, were typical livestock holdings. Cotton production, on average, rose only slightly among these farmers. Whitesides, however, was an exception. He raised twelve 450-pound bales in 1870, while Oates raised six and Sinclair five.[11] This evidence suggests that those who turned quickly to cash-crop production made a more rapid recovery than those who delayed.

One final cause contributed to the slow economic recovery: the labor supply. Obviously, those who had used slave labor before the war had to depend on themselves or hired laborers. There was, in fact, a large increase in the amount of hired labor reported in 1870 over what had been reported in 1860. One reason was that some men had returned from the war in ill health. Also by 1870, a significant number of Pisgah households were headed by widows. The loss of men in such numbers had implications not only for farm management but for church life as well, for in a patriarchal society like that at Pisgah, not only church leadership but religious instruction at home rested largely with the male population. In this latter respect the state of the economy and the condition of the church clearly intersected. Though economics figured prominently in Oates's assessment of the church after thirty years, he realized that there were problems that beset Pisgah that went beyond the material.

Oates's main concern upon his arrival at Pisgah was rebuilding the church congregation. From the outset, one feature of Oates's ministry was his frequent visits among his congregation. Those who knew him remarked about his willingness to mount his horse and ride to see the members. He was also known for taking "frequent and long trips on horseback to visit vacancies. For some years he paid a visit annually to Prosperity and New Hope—a horseback ride of several days through mountainous country."[12] Early in his ministry, Oates confronted certain problems that needed remedy or resolution. The church structure, which had deteriorated during the war, needed repairs, but it was 1869 before the congregation could afford them. The economic austerity prevented the congregation's adequate support of the work of the church. Only four members, he found, subscribed to the church paper, which meant that the people were not well informed about the work of the church as they would have been in earlier times. But perhaps the most complex and trying problem was lingering animosities engendered by the war and the dissatisfaction that had erupted among the members during the conflict. The tension in the church was relieved to some extent when Mount Zion Church was established in 1870 and some disaffected Pisgah members withdrew to that church.[13] However, try as Oates and his congregation might, postwar Pisgah could not reclaim its prewar cohesion.

Though the economy slowly recovered, the Pisgah community as a whole would not regain the prosperity, material well-being, and social and religious unity that had characterized it on the eve of the war. The people's displacement, their reduction to poverty, the large number of casualties among Pisgah's fighting men, postwar animosities and economic struggle, and the continued loss of the founders—the patriarchs and matriarchs of the colony—through death had loosed Pisgah Church's hold on the people as the center of their community. Members who had arrived as children in the 1850s came of age, married, and began their own families. They began to scatter in pursuit of land and a living. By 1870, there were more than 400 Pisgah people in Pope County, for the most part in Illinois and Galley Rock townships. Of those identified, 350 were white and 78 black, 22 of the latter bearing the name McElwee.[14]

By that time, too, there had been a general population shift away from the area surrounding Pisgah Church toward the river. For convenience, Sabbath school began informally at the Galla Creek School about three miles to the south soon after Monroe Oates arrived at Pisgah. In 1872, "more formal work" began there. For several years services were held there as well as at Pisgah. Because the Sabbath school was better attended than at Pisgah and the attendance at public worship was good as well, it was decided to build another church in that area. Monroe Oates oversaw the construction of Bethany Church in 1877, a frame house thirty by fifty feet.[15]

In 1878 or 1879, the church attained a membership of 116, the highest number since before the war. For the next five years, however, membership declined. While Bethany served the members of the congregation who lived east of Galley Creek and south toward the river, Pisgah continued to serve those to the north and west of the Creek, but declined in membership through deaths and removals. Other members had moved to Potts Station and its vicinity, which had begun to grow after the railroad came through in the early 1870s. It was decided to build a church at Potts Station. Oates preached the first sermon there on the first Sabbath in March 1884 and served both the Pottsville Church and Bethany Church for the next sixteen years.[16] Though Pisgah Church was no longer used, its congregation continued at Pottsville.

After thirty years Oates looked back on his ministry at Pisgah with some satisfaction. Once the early postwar years had passed, unity had prevailed, "except in one case when the Grange was in operation, but that passed away without any serious results."[17] Although Oates does not discuss the point of the controversy, it was most likely a reflection on the social and political controversies surrounding the agricultural protest movements of the late nineteenth century. Oates credited "the unanimity and harmony that has prevailed between the members of the church" to the blood relationship among them. "When the members of the church are of one mind and work together," he wrote, "they can accomplish a great deal, but if they are divided and antagonize each other, they are liable to become paralyzed, and accomplish little good for the cause of Christ."[18]

There were other reasons to be thankful. The saloons had been closed, subscribers to the church paper greatly increased, and people were generally better informed on the work of the church. Monetary contributions to that work had steadily grown, and there had been an increase in the number of people willing to participate in the public prayer meetings.[19]

But Oates also counted what he saw as his and his congregation's failings, and in them one gains a hint here and there of how the church that Oates ministered to differed from that of prewar Pisgah. The church had not grown dramatically during his ministry. It had grown until the late 1870s, when its membership peaked at 116. Then it declined for a number of years as a result of deaths and removals. By 1898, when Oates was assessing his career, membership had recovered and gained to 120. Of those, only eleven were there when he came to Pisgah, among them only three of the founding members. The new generations were apparently not like the founders. As the century drew near its close, Oates found a general disregard to duty among heads of family in conducting family worship in their homes. Not only he, but the elders and the members were not giving proper attention to duty in visiting the sick and counseling the impenitent. But perhaps the most telling failure was this: "Another mistake we have made detrimental to the interests of the church was parting with the inheritances of the Fathers, and letting them pass into the hands of strangers. The sons and daughters of the church have parted with much valuable real estate, and located in other places without improving their temporal condition, to the great loss of the mother church. But we should not regret this if they are instrumental in building up the church in other places."[20] Nor, one might add, should he have regretted it if their removal had improved their temporal condition.

Oates's contemporaries were less critical of his efforts than he was, especially concerning removals from the church. One wrote, "Nearly all of the members of Russellville, Zion, and Little Rock went from this church. What he has done for the A. R. P. church in Arkansas it is impossible to tell. He has helped to hold together the A. R. P. churches in this state."[21] Nearly a century has passed since Oates assessed his congregation and his work among them. Viewed from the present perspective, one might consider the out migration of the postwar generations a repetition, in their own way, of what their progenitors had done. After all, their history since the seventeenth century had been one of migration: for many, Scotland to Ireland to Pennsylvania to the Carolinas to Arkansas. The late-nineteenth-century Pisgah people, too, sought a land where they could better provide for their families and improve their opportunities.

In the twentieth century, with the urbanization of America and the advent of the technological era, the out migrations continued. But no matter how far they are separated from Pisgah by geography or elapsed generations, most who descend from the original settlers possess a good deal of detailed knowledge of what their ancestors did. Many make pilgrimages to Pisgah Cemetery. There, as they walk on its well-kept grounds, read the names of patriarchs and matriarchs of Pisgah chiseled in the stones, stand at the crest of the hill where the old church stood, and look at the vista spread before them, they sense the strength of will, determination, and faith that sent the people from established homes in search of a land and brought them to that place, where they believed they could build a community that would foster the temporal and spiritual well-being of their children. Standing on the crest of the hill, looking north toward Crow Mountain and west to Mount Nebo, their descendants gain a renewed sense of what a remarkable event the covered-wagon migrations to Pisgah were in the social and religious history of nineteenth-century America.

# Notes

## Chapter 1 ❀ They Sought a Land

1. Franklin Knox Oates, "Early History of the Oates and Related Families."

2. Robert B. Elliott Jr., *A History*, 11.

3. John Willson to Alexander Wear, April 25, 1842.

4. Moses Wilson to Alexander Wear, April 30, 1842.

5. *Gastonia Gazette*, January 10, 1934.

6. Lora Beth Henry Rogers, "The History and Genealogy"; Elliott, *A History*, 11.

7. James A. Bradley to Alexander Wear, September 15, 1842; ibid.

8. Ibid.

9. Ibid.

10. Ibid.

11. Bradley to Wear, November 16, 1846.

12. Ibid.

13. Elliott, *A History*, 13.

14. A number of sources were useful in the foregoing and subsequent brief sketches of Associate Reformed Presbyterian Church history. A bare outline is provided by R. M. Stevenson, *Studies*. A detailed but scattered treatment appears in Robert Lathan, *History*, especially the first seven chapters. By far the most readable and helpful source is Ray A. King, *History*, especially chapters one and two. Also helpful but less accessible is King, "Study," especially 1–25.

15. Stevenson, *Studies*, 19.

16. Elliott, *A History*, 2–4.

17. Wilma Dykeman, *With Fire and Sword*, 1–12; Jane Gaston Kitchens, *The History*, 2–3.

18. Elliott, *A History*, 4.

19. Ibid., 5.

20. Ibid., 8–9; E. E. Boyce, "Historical Sketch."

# Chapter 2 ✳ The First Migrations, 1850–1852

1. Neill H. Bell, "History of the Pottsville-Bethany Church."

2. Monroe Oates, "History of Pisgah Church, Arkansas."

3. Calvin Grier Oates, "Biographical Sketch of John Oates, Sr."

4. Ibid.

5. *Arkansas State Gazette and Democrat,* September 13, 1850.

6. U.S. Census, Population Schedules, 1850, Pope County, Arkansas.

7. Bell, "History of the Pottsville-Bethany Church."

8. Neill H. Bell, "Pottsville-Bethany Associate Reformed Presbyterian Church," 11.

9. *Arkansas State Gazette and Democrat,* April 5 and 12, May 10, 17, and 31, June 7, and September 13, 1850.

10. Franklin Knox Oates, "Early History of the Oates and Related Families."

11. Calvin Grier Oates, "Biographical Sketch."

12. Mrs. Marvin Williamson and Neill H. Bell, "The Oates Family," 2.

13. Monroe Oates, "History"; Calvin Grier Oates, "Biographical Sketch"; Pope County Tax Records, 1852.

14. *Centennial History,* 64–65

15. U.S. Census, Slave Schedules, 1850, Gaston County, North Carolina; Pope County Tax Records, 1852.

16. Williamson and Bell, "The Oates Family," 6.

17. Ibid.; Monroe Oates, "History."

18. Laban Miles Hoffman, *Our Kin,* 63, 64, 104–6; U.S. Census, Slave Schedules, 1850, Gaston County, North Carolina.

19. Pope County Deed Records, D-119, D-144, D-181, D-280; Calvin Grier Oates, "Biographical Sketch."

20. Monroe Oates, "History."

21. U.S. Census, Slave Schedules, 1850, Gaston County, North Carolina; Jane Sinclair Ferguson, comp., "Ancestry of the Family of Ferguson."

22. Ferguson, "Ancestry."

23. Ibid.; Andrew N. Falls to Alexander Weir, February 7, 1853; Monroe Oates, "History."

24. Pope County Will Records, 1852.

25. Ferguson, "Ancestry"; Christinia Smith Ferguson, "Ferguson"; Dorcas Ferguson Patterson and Alice Ann Harris, "The Ferguson Family History," 224.

26. Falls to Weir, February 7, 1853

27. Monroe Oates, "History"; Falls to Weir, February 7, 1853.

28. *Centennial History*, 269.

29. Ibid.

30. Ray A. King, *History*, 86–88.

31. Ibid., 84, 85.

32. King, "Study," 63–69.

33. *Centennial History*, 270.

34. *Minutes of the Associate Reformed Synod of the South* (1853), 34.

35. Monroe Oates, "A Sketch."

36. Monroe Oates, "History."

37. Lathan, *History*, 415.

38. *The Constitution and Standards of the Associate Reformed Presbyterian Church in North America*, Sec. III.

39. Ibid.

40. *Minutes of the Associate Reformed Synod of the South* (1853), 34, 35.

41. Falls to Weir, February 7, 1853.

# Chapter 3 ❊ Building a Community, 1853–1855

1. Falls to Weir, February 7, 1853.

2. Pinckney Glasgow McElwee, comp., *Genealogy of William McElwee, II*, 2

3. Katie Murdoch, "William L. McElwee"; William Hood, "A Classmate on Rev. M. Oates"; "Elizabeth Oates & Thomas Oates (March 22, 1860)," 73–74.

4. Hood, "A Classmate."

5. Pope County Deed Records, E-39.

6. Thomas M. Oates to A. Wear and Family, March 9, 1854.

7. Pope County Deed Records, E-18.

8. Pope County Deed Records.

9. Oates to Wier and Family, March 9, 1854.

10. Ibid.

11. Ruth Bell Wharton, "Alexander Kidd Dickey," 213–14.

12. Neill H. Bell, "The Family of Alexander and Mary Oates Bell," 1; Wharton, "Alexander Bell," 145.

13. Monroe Oates, "History."

14. Pope County Tax Records, 1854.

15. E. B. Sinclair, "Gregory Sinclair," 422; Thomas G. Sinclair, "Samuel Sinclair," 379–80.

16. Elta Falls Houser, "Sinclair Saga."

17. Ibid.

18. Ibid.; Bell, "Family Notes."

19. Houser, "Sinclair Saga."

20. Ibid.; Bell, "Family Notes."

21. Mary Ann Sinclair Falls, "Family Tree, or History."

22. E. B. Sinclair, "Gregory Sinclair," 422; *Weekly Tribune,* July 16, 1936.

23. Houser, "Sinclair Saga"; Bell, "Family Notes."

24. Falls, "Family Tree, or History"; Pope County Deed Records, E-301.

25. Ernie Dean, "105 Year Old Sinclair House."

26. Falls, "Family Tree, or History."

27. Monroe Oates, "History."

28. Ibid.

29. Ibid.

30. Lathan, *History,* 416–17.

31. Ibid., 417.

32. *Constitution and Standards of the Associate Reformed Presbyterian Church in North America,* Sec. III. For the atmosphere of Communion, I am deeply indebted to J. W. Stevenson's book *God in My Unbelief.* Stevenson wrote about the atmosphere of Communion in an obscure parish (Crainie) in Scotland. It struck me because it was somewhat like the atmosphere at my home during the Communion time. My mother came out of the heart of the Pisgah tradition. Accordingly, this may have been similar to the atmosphere of Pisgah.

33. Monroe Oates, "History."

34. *Minutes of the Associate Reformed Synod* (1854), 15; *Minutes of the Associate Reformed Synod* (1855), 14.

35. Pope County Deed Records, F-95.

## Chapter 4 ❋ Economic Prosperity

1. W. Gene Boyett, *Hardscrabble Frontier,* 8.

2. Falls to Weir, February 7, 1853; Boyett, *Hardscrabble Frontier,* 8.

3. *Arkansas State Gazette and Democrat,* January 9, 1852, and July 25 and December 27, 1857; J. R. Homer Scott to Henry C. Scott, July 25, 1851, and May 4, 1852, Nancy Scott and J. R. Homer Scott to H. C. Scott, September 16, 1855, and Nancy Scott to H. C. Scott, November 11, 1853, Scott Family Letters; Boyett, *Hardscrabble Frontier,* 25, 27, 28.

4. George S. Scott to Henry C. Scott, May 29, 1853, Scott Family Letters.

5. J. R. Homer Scott to Henry C. Scott, July 26, 1854, Scott Family Letters.

6. Ibid., December 7, 1854.

7. Ibid., June 1, 1855, and July 25, 1857.

8. Nancy Scott to Henry Scott, October 6, 1857, Scott Family Letters.

9. C. C. Ewing to William G. Ewing, July 20, 1858, Ewing Family Letters; *Arkansas State Gazette and Democrat,* January 2, 1858; Boyett, *Hardscrabble Frontier,* 9.

10. Ibid. 18.

11. Ibid.; U.S. Agricultural Census, 1860, Pope County, Arkansas.

12. Boyett, *Hardscrabble Frontier,* 20, 25, 26; U.S. Agricultural Census, 1860, Pope County, Arkansas.

13. Boyett, *Hardscrabble Frontier,* 23–24; U.S. Agricultural Census, 1860, Pope County, Arkansas.

14. Boyett, *Hardscrabble Frontier,* 21–22; U.S. Agricultural Census, 1860, Pope County, Arkansas.

15. Boyett, *Hardscrabble Frontier,* 21–22.

16. J. B. Lemley, "Negroes in Pope County," 34; U.S. Census, Slave Schedules, 1860, Pope County, Arkansas; U.S. Agricultural Census, 1860, Pope County, Arkansas.

17. See, for example, *Arkansas State Gazette and Democrat,* February 6, March 19, April 2, and June 18, 1852; June 2, 1854; April 19, May 31, and June 28, 1856.

18. Alexander Bell to M. C. Bell, July 8, 1856.

19. *Arkansas State Gazette and Democrat,* April 18, 1857; J. R. Homer Scott to George Scott, June 14, 1857, Scott Family Letters.

20. Nancy Dickey to Mary Ann McGill, May 18, 1858.

21. J. R. Homer Scott to Henry C. Scott, June 17, 1859, Scott Family Letters; C. C. Ewing to Elizabeth Ewing, May 8, 1860, Ewing Family Letters.

22. *Arkansas State Gazette and Democrat,* February 13 and 20, 1852; Pope County Deed Records, D-135.

23. J. R. Homer Scott to Henry C. Scott, May 4, 1852, Scott Family Letters; *Arkansas State Gazette and Democrat,* May 14, 1852.

24. Alexander Bell to M. C. Bell, July 8, 1856; J. R. Homer Scott to George Scott, June 14, 1857, and J. R. Homer Scott to Henry C. Scott, June 1, 1855, Scott Family Letters.

25. J. R. Homer Scott to Henry C. Scott, May 4, 1852, Scott Family Letters.

26. Oates to Weer and Family, March 9, 1854; Alexander Bell to M. C. Bell, July 8, 1856.

27. J. R. Homer Scott to George Scott, June 14, 1857, Scott Family Letters.

28. C. C. Ewing to Elizabeth Ewing, October 30, 1858, Ewing Family Letters.

29. Boyett, *Hardscrabble Frontier,* 18.

30. J. R. Homer Scott to Henry C. Scott, April 16, 1856, and May 4, 1852, Scott Family Letters.

31. U.S. Agricultural Census, 1860, Pope County, Arkansas; Ruby S. Harkey, "An Interview with Mary Ann Sinclair Falls."

32. Nancy Dickey to Mary Ann McGill, May 18, 1858.

33. J. R. Homer Scott to Henry Scott, August 21, 1858, and December 14, 1858, Scott Family Letters.

34. J. R. Homer Scott to Henry Scott, August 21, 1858, Scott Family Letters; Harkey, "An Interview."

35. U.S. Agricultural Census, 1860, Pope County, Arkansas.

36. Boyett, *Hardscrabble Frontier,* 6, 142.

37. U.S. Census, Population Schedules, 1860, Pope County, Arkansas.

38. Boyett, *Hardscrabble Frontier,* 8; Nancy Scott to Henry C. Scott, January 10, 1858, Scott Family Letters; *Arkansas State Gazette and Democrat,* January 2, 1858; Pope County Tax Records, 1860.

39. Pope County Tax Records, 1860.

40. Boyett, *Hardscrabble Frontier,* 31.

41. U.S. Census, Slave Schedules, 1860, Pope County, Arkansas; Pope County Tax Records, 1860.

42. Pope County Tax Records, 1860.

43. Boyett, *Hardscrabble Frontier,* 125.

44. Lincoln County (Tennessee) Will Records, 1847; Monroe Oates, "Mr. A. N. Falls."

# Chapter 5 ✻ "Carolina" in Pope County

1. Boyett, *Hardscrabble Frontier*, 6–7; Alexander Bell to M. C. Bell, July 8, 1856.

2. Ibid.

3. Elliott, *A History*, 13–14.

4. Alexander Bell to M. C. Bell, July 8, 1856.

5. Ruth Bell Wharton, "Alexander Dickey, Sr."; *Biographical and Historical Memoirs of Western Arkansas*, 224.

6. Wharton, "Alexander Kidd Dickey," 214.

7. "The Henry Family Has a Reunion"; *Biographical and Historical Memoirs of Western Arkansas*, 232–33.

8. J. A. Henry, "Silas Alexander Henry," 262; "The Henry Family Has a Reunion."

9. Ernestine Allmon McKinney, "The William and Isabella McKeown Henry Family"; Henry, "Silas Alexander Henry," 262.

10. Dorcas Ferguson Patterson and Alice Ann Harris, "The Henry Family History," 260; Mrs. William Henry, Interview; "The Henry Family."

11. "Henry Reunion Enjoyed by Many Families"; *Biographical and Historical Memoirs of Western Arkansas*, 233–34.

12. Lora Beth Henry Rogers, "Arkansas Covered Wagon Pioneers"; *Miss Elsie Oates' Scrap-Book*, 13.

13. Rogers, "Arkansas Covered Wagon Pioneers."

14. *Molly Falls' Scrapbooks*, 252.

15. Rogers, "Arkansas Covered Wagon Pioneers."

16. Margaret Oates Goodman to William O. Ragsdale, June 2, 1992; Pope County Tax Records, 1860.

17. *Molly Falls' Scrapbooks*, 108.

18. Goodman to Ragsdale, June 2, 1992.

19. Monroe Oates, "History."

20. *Biographical and Historical Memoirs of Western Arkansas*, 242–43; Carl F. Parker, "The Parker Family History," 267.

21. *Molly Falls' Scrapbooks*, 158.

22. Ibid.; Hannah Haw Lewis Scott, "The Anthony Family," 212.

23. Scott, "The Anthony Family," 212.

24. Marion Peeler LaVasque, "Capt. William M. Peeler," 370; *Biographical and Historical Memoirs of Western Arkansas,* 243; Niva Daniels Rice, "The Daniels Family."

25. Weir to Bradley, January 11, 1859.

26. Ibid.

27. Monroe Oates, "History."

28. *Centennial History,* 25.

29. Monroe Oates, "History."

30. *Centennial History,* 262.

31. Ibid., 270, 551; *Minutes of the Associate Reformed Synod* (1860), 13, 38.

32. *Minutes of the Associate Reformed Synod* (1860), 38.

33. Mona L. Cowan to W. O. Ragsdale, April 1991; *Centennial History,* 551; *Minutes of the Associate Reformed Synod* (1860), 38.

34. *Minutes of the Associate Reformed Synod* (1860), 38, 39; "Associate Reformed Presbyterian Church of Pottsville."

35. *Centennial History,* 189–90.

36. Ibid., 213, 489, 515, 520–21, 555, 571.

37. Maggie Bell, "Pottsville and Bethany Associate Reformed Presbyterian Churches."

38. *Centennial History,* 13; Monroe Oates, "History"; Calvin Grier Oates, "Biographical Sketch."

39. Monroe Oates, "A Sketch of Thirty Years."

40. Monroe Oates, "History."

# Chapter 6 ❊ Pisgah in the Civil War

1. See, for example, *Arkansas State Gazette and Democrat,* September 1 and 29, 1860.

2. J. R. H. Scott to George and Henry Scott, May 10, 1861, Scott Family Letters.

3. Cyrus C. Ewing to Dear Sister, Summer, 1866, Ewing Family Letters.

4. Missouri Ewing to Elizabeth Ewing, April 7, 1860, Ewing Family Letters.

5. Williamson and Bell, "The Oates Family."

6. King, *History,* 84, 85, 86–88; Lathan, *History,* 300–301; Elliott, *A History,* 10.

7. King, *History,* 111.

8. Lathan, *History*, 367.

9. King, *History*, 111–12.

10. Ibid., 112.

11. See, for example, "Elizabeth Oates & Thomas Oates (March 22, 1860)."

12. Pope County Will Records, 1855.

13. Bell, "The Family of Alex and Mary Bell," 2.

14. Wesley Thurman Leeper, *Rebels Valiant,* 15–16.

15. Ibid., 34, 40–41; John C. Stroud, "Gally Rock Men," 55.

16. *Molly Falls' Scrapbooks,* 252; Laban Miles Hoffman, *Our Kin,* 106; "Pope County Company 'B,'" 57; Stroud, "Gally Rock Men," 55.

17. Leeper, *Rebels Valiant,* 49, 52, 58, 61.

18. J. B. Lemley, "Company F," 56.

19. "Pope County Company 'B,'" 56; Ferguson, "Ancestry"; *Molly Falls' Scrapbooks,* 342; Calvin Grier Oates, "Biographical Sketch"; Carl F. Parker, "James Whitesides."

20. Leeper, *Rebels Valiant,* 84.

21. J. A. Henry, "Silas Alexander Henry," 262; *Biographical and Historical Memoirs of Western Arkansas,* 268.

22. Leeper, *Rebels Valiant,* 139.

23. S. C. Tucker Jr., "Crow Mountain Volunteers," 86–88; Lora Beth Henry Rogers, "History and Genealogy."

24. "Pope County Company 'B,'" 56–57.

25. Leeper, *Rebels Valiant,* 291–92; Henry, "Original Roster of Company 'B,'" 58–59.

26. A. W. Henry to Dear Wife, Mother & Sisters, March 19, 1864 ; Wallace Hughey to W. O. Ragsdale, September 22, 1994.

27. Bell, "The Family of Alex and Mary Bell," 2–3.

28. Rogers, "Arkansas Covered Wagon Pioneers"; Rogers to W. O. Ragsdale, July 17, 1991.

29. Cyrus C. Ewing to Dear Sister, Summer, 1866, Ewing Family Letters.

30. Pope County Deed Records, I-184; Noah Cooper to T. C. McRae, February 3, 1902.

31. Carl F. Parker, "Analysis," 45–49.

32. Lemley, "Home Guards Appointed," 54–55.

# Chapter 7 ❋ The Pisgah Home Front in War and Reconstruction

1. Mrs. William (Mae Dell Brown) Simmons, comp., "Genealogy of Hollinger Daniel Brown, Jr."; Mary Ann Sinclair Falls, "History of the Falls Family."

2. S. C. Tucker Jr., *To Sell a Good Bull,* 40–41.

3. Falls, "Family Tree, or History"; Elta Falls Houser, "Sinclair Saga."

4. C. C. Ewing to William G. Ewing, April 10, 1866, and Ewing to Dear Sister, Summer, 1866, Ewing Family Letters.

5. Houser, "Falls Family History."

6. Tucker, *To Sell a Good Bull,* 40.

7. *Miss Elsie Oates' Scrap-Book,* 34; Wade Oates, Interview.

8. Falls, "Family Tree, or History."

9. Houser, "Sinclair Saga."

10. Simmons, "Genealogy of Hollinger Daniel Brown, Jr."

11. A. W. Henry to Dear Wife, Mother & Sisters, March 14, 1864, copy in author's file provided by Wallace Hughey; Henry to Dear Wife and Dear Mother, November 27, 1857, copy in author's file provided by Wallace Hughey.

12. John M. Bradley to Sarah Caroline Bradley, February 12, 1865.

13. Ibid.

14. Houser, "Falls Family History."

15. Rogers, "Arkansas Covered Wagon Pioneers."

16. Bell, "The Family of Alex and Mary Bell," 2.

17. Tucker, *To Sell a Good Bull,* 43.

18. H. P. Barry, untitled article, *Dardanelle Post Dispatch.*

19. Houser, "Falls Family History"; U.S. Agricultural Census, 1860, Pope County, Arkansas.

20. Barry, untitled article, *Dardanelle Post Dispatch.*

21. William Bowen to W. O. Ragsdale, September 20, 1990.

22. "Arkansas Mounted Rifles"; Joe D. Henry, "Silas A. Henry."

23. *Biographical and Historical Memoirs of Western Arkansas,* 242–43; Parker, "The Parker Family History," 368; U.S. Agricultural Census, 1860, Pope County, Arkansas.

24. John M. Bradley to Sarah Caroline Bradley, February 12, 1865.

25. Calvin Grier Oates, "Biographical Sketch."

26. Barry, untitled article, *Dardanelle Post Dispatch.*

27. Ibid.

28. Cyrus C. Ewing to William G. Ewing, April 10, 1866, Ewing Family Letters.

29. Ibid.

30. Cyrus C. Ewing to Dear Sister, Summer, 1866; Cyrus C. Ewing to William G. Ewing, April 10, 1866, and February 19, 1867, Ewing Family Letters.

31. Ibid.

32. William Marvin Hurley, "Socializing Forces," 35, 36; *Arkansas Gazette,* September 1, 1866.

33. *Arkansas Gazette,* September 1 and 29, 1866.

34. Hurley, "Socializing Forces," 36.

35. Cyrus C. Ewing to William G. Ewing, February 19, 1867, Ewing Family Letters.

36. Ibid.; Cyrus C. Ewing to William G. Ewing, November 5, 1867, Ewing Family Letters.

37. Monroe Oates, "A Sketch."

38. *Centennial History,* 571–72.

39. For a history of attempts at union, see Ray A. King, "Analysis," 100–114.

40. Monroe Oates, "A Sketch."

41. Monroe Oates, "History."

42. Ibid.

43. *Molly Falls' Scrapbooks,* 339.

44. Calvin Grier Oates, "Biographical Sketch."

45. Monroe Oates, "A Sketch."

46. Monroe Oates, "History."

47. Ibid.

48. Ibid.

49. Monroe Oates, "A Sketch."

50. Ibid.

51. *Centennial History,* 190.

52. Monroe Oates, "History."

53. *Centennial History,* 270.

54. Ibid., 229, 555.

55. Monroe Oates, "A Sketch."

# Chapter 8 ✳ Rebuilding Pisgah

1. John W. Carson, "Father Oates."

2. Hood, "A Classmate on Rev. M. Oates."

3. Carson, "Father Oates"; *Centennial History*, 262.

4. Carson, "Father Oates"; *Centennial History*, 225.

5. Carson, "Father Oates"; *Centennial History*, 263.

6. Carson, "Father Oates."

7. Monroe Oates, "History."

8. Monroe Oates, "A Sketch."

9. Ashmore, *Arkansas*, 97.

10. Pope County Tax Records, 1860 and 1870.

11. Ibid.; U.S. Agricultural Census, 1860 and 1870, Pope County, Arkansas.

12. *Centennial History*, 263.

13. Monroe Oates, "A Sketch"; M. G. Hearn, "Reminiscences of the Old Mt. Zion Church."

14. U.S. Census, Population Schedules, 1870, Pope County, Arkansas.

15. Monroe Oates, "History."

16. Ibid.; "Pisgah-Bethany-Pottsville."

17. Monroe Oates, "A Sketch."

18. Ibid.

19. Ibid.

20. Ibid.

21. Carson, "Father Oates."

# Sources

"Arkansas Mounted Rifles," *Courier-Democrat* (Russellville, AR). Undated clipping, copy in author's file.

*Arkansas State Gazette and Democrat,* 1850–1866.

Ashmore, Harry S. *Arkansas, a Bicentennial History.* New York: Norton, 1978.

"Associate Reformed Presbyterian Church of Pottsville, Pope County, Arkansas." 1978. Unpublished typescript, copy in author's file.

Barry, H. P. Untitled article, *Dardanelle Post Dispatch.* Vertical file, Arkansas Valley Regional Library, Dardanelle, Arkansas.

Bell, Alexander, to M. C. Bell, July 8, 1856. Copy in author's file.

Bell, Maggie. "Pottsville and Bethany Associate Reformed Presbyterian Churches," *Associate Reformed Presbyterian,* January 27, 1943.

———. "History of the Pottsville-Bethany Church," *Associate Reformed Presbyterian,* November 11, 1956.

Bell, Neill H.. "Pottsville-Bethany Associate Reformed Presbyterian Church," *Arkansas Valley Historical Papers,* No. 17 (August 1958), 9–12.

———. "The Family of Alex and Mary Bell," *Arkansas Valley Historical Papers,* No. 19 (September 1959), 1–8.

———. "Family Notes." 1962. Unpublished typescript, copy in author's file.

*Biographical and Historical Memoirs of Western Arkansas.* Chicago: Southern Publishing Co., 1891.

Bowen, William, to W. O. Ragsdale, September 20, 1990. Copy in author's file.

Boyce, E. E. "Historical Sketch of the Associate Reformed Presbyterian Church at Bethany, York District, South Carolina," *Associate Reformed Presbyterian,* February 21, 1934, reprinted from *Religious Telescope,* 1859.

Boyett, W. Gene. *Hardscrabble Frontier: Pope County, Arkansas in the 1850's.* Lanham, MD: University Press of America, Inc., 1990.

Bradley, James A., to Alexander Wear, September 15, 1842, and November 16, 1846. Copy in author's file provided by Mrs. Moffatt Ware.

Bradley, John M., to Sarah Caroline Bradley, February 12, 1865. Copy in author's file provided by Lora Beth Henry Rogers.

Carson, John. "Father Oates," *Associate Reformed Presbyterian,* November 28, 1900.

*The Centennial History of the Associate Reformed Presbyterian Church, 1803–1903.* Charleston, SC: Walker, Evans, & Cogswell Co., 1905.

*The Constitution and Standards of the Associate Reformed Presbyterian Church in North America.* Pittsburgh: Johnston and Stockton, 1827.

Cooper, Noah, to T. C. McRae, February 3, 1902. Manuscripts, Arkansas History Commission.

Cowan, Mona L., to W. O. Ragsdale, April 1991. Copy in author's file.

Dean, Ernie. "105 Year Old Sinclair House Is Russellville Landmark," *Arkansas Gazette.* Undated clipping, copy in author's file.

Dickey, Nancy, to Mary Ann McGill, May 18, 1858. Copy in author's file provided by Mrs. Moffatt Ware.

Dykeman, Wilma. *With Fire and Sword: The Battle of Kings Mountain.* Washington, D.C.: U.S. Department of the Interior, 1978.

"Elizabeth Oates & Thomas Oates (March 22, 1860)," *Pope County Historical Association Quarterly* 5 (June 1971): 73–75.

Elliott, Robert B., Jr. *A History of Pisgah Associate Reformed Presbyterian Church, Gastonia, N.C.* 1971. Reprint ed. Kings Mountain, NC: The Printin' Press, 1996.

Ewing Family Letters. Copies in author's file provided by Mona L. Cowan.

Falls, Andrew N., to Alexander Weir, February 7, 1853. Copy in author's file provided by Mrs. Moffatt Ware.

Falls, Mary Ann Sinclair. "Family Tree, or History." 1926. Unpublished typescript, copy in author's file.

Ferguson, Christinia Smith. "Ferguson." 1989. Unpublished typescript, copy in author's file.

Ferguson, Jane Sinclair. "Ancestry of the Family of Ferguson." Unpublished typescript, copy in author's file.

*Gastonia Gazette* (Gastonia, NC), 1934.

Goodman, Margaret Oates, to William O. Ragsdale, June 2, 1992. Copy in author's file.

Harkey, Ruby S. "An Interview with Mary Ann Sinclair Falls," April 18, 1941. Unpublished typescript, copy in author's file.

Hearn, M. G. "Reminiscences of the Old Mt. Zion Church," *Courier Democrat,* May 5, 1910.

Henry, A. W., to Dear Wife and Dear Mother, November 27, 1857, and Henry to Dear Wife, Mother & Sisters, March 19, 1864. Copy in author's file provided by Wallace Hughey.

Henry, J. A. "Original Roster of Company 'B'," in *History of Pope County, Arkansas* (Topeka, KS: Josten's Publishing Co., 1981), 58–59.

———. "Silas Alexander Henry," in *History of Pope County, Arkansas* (Winston-Salem, NC: Hunter Publishing Co., 1979), 262.

Henry, Joe D. "Silas A. Henry." 1962. Unpublished typescript, copy in author's file.

Henry, Mrs. William. Interview, Pottsville, Arkansas, January 5, 1946. Transcript in author's file.

"The Henry Family," *Arkansas Valley Historical Papers,* No. 5 (November 1954), 4–9.

The Henry Family Has a Reunion," *Courier-Democrat.* Undated [1926] clipping, copy in author's file.

"Henry Reunion Enjoyed by Many Families." Undated newspaper clipping, copy in author's file.

Hoffman, Laban Miles. *Our Kin, Being a History of the Hoffman, Rhyne, Costner, Rudisill, Best, Hoves, Hoyle, Wills, Shetley, Jenkins, Holland, Hambright, Gaston, Withers, Cansler, Clemmer and Linberger Families.* 1915; reprint ed. Baltimore, MD: Gateway Press, Inc., 1980.

Hood, William. "A Classmate on Rev. M. Oates," *Associate Reformed Presbyterian,* November 28, 1900.

Houser, Elta Falls. "History of the Falls Family." 1929. Unpublished typescript, copy in author's file.

———. "Falls Family History." Unpublished typescript, copy in author's file.

———. "Sinclair Saga." Unpublished typescript, copy in author's file.

Hughey, Wallace, to W. O. Ragsdale, September 22, 1994. Copy in author's file.

Hurley, William Marvin. "Socializing Forces in the History of Pope County, Arkansas." Master's thesis, University of Arkansas, Fayetteville, 1931.

King, Ray A. *A History of the Associate Reformed Presbyterian Church.* Charlotte, NC: Board of Christian Education of the Associate Reformed Presbyterian Church, 1966.

———. "A Study of the Ecumenical Relations of the Associate Reformed Synod of the South, 1822–1912." Master of Theology thesis. Austin Presbyterian Theological Seminary, 1970.

Kitchens, Jane Gaston. *The History of Union Associate Reformed Presbyterian*

*Church, 1745–1967, Richburg, Chester County, South Carolina.* Richburg, SC: Author, 1967.

Lathan, Robert. *History of the Associate Reformed Synod of the South, to Which Is Prefixed a History of the Associate Presbyterian and Reformed Presbyterian Chruches.* 1882; reprint ed. Charlotte, NC: Washburn Press, 1979.

LaVasque, Marion Peeler. "Capt. William M. Peeler," in *History of Pope County, Arkansas* (Winston-Salem, NC: Hunter Publishing Co., 1979), 370.

Leeper, Wesley Thurman. *Rebels Valiant: Second Arkansas Mounted Rifles (Dismounted).* Little Rock, AR: Pioneer Press, 1964.

Lemley, J. B. "Company F, 1st Battalion, Arkansas Cavalry," in *History of Pope County, Arkansas* (Topeka, KS: Josten's Publishing Co., 1981), 56.

———. "Home Guards Appointed," in *History of Pope County, Arkansas* (Topeka, KS: Josten's Publishing Co., 1981), 54–55.

———. "Negroes in Pope County," in *History of Pope County, Arkansas* (Topeka, KS: Josten's Publishing Co., 1981), 34–35.

Lincoln County (Tennessee) Will Records.

McElwee, Pinckney Glasgow, comp. *Genealogy of William McElwee, II of Clarks Fork of Bullocks Creek of York County, South Carolina.* 1959; reprint ed. Waxahatchie, TX: Mrs. Gary W. Oates, 1978.

McKinney, Ernestine Allmon. "The William and Isabella McKeown Henry Family of York District, South Carolina." 1939. Unpublished typescript, copy in author's file.

*Minutes of the Associate Reformed Synod of the South, Held at Mount Olivet, Bath Co., Ky., October 10, 1853.* Due West, SC: Telescope, 1853.

*Minutes of the Associate Reformed Synod of the South, Held at Hopewell, Chester District, S.C., October 9, 1854.* Due West, SC: Telescope, 1854.

*Minutes of the Associate Reformed Synod of the South, Held at Cedar Spring, Abbeville District, S.C., October 8, 9, 10 & 11, 1855.* Due West, SC: Telescope, 1855.

*Minutes of the Associate Reformed Synod of the South Held at Hopewell, Newton County, Georgia, October 8th, 9th, 10, 1860.* Due West, SC: "Telescope" Power Press, 1860.

*Miss Elsie Oates' Scrap-Book.* Elaine Weir Cia, ed. Little Rock, AR: n.p., 1978.

*Molly Falls' Scrapbooks.* Elaine Weir Cia and Jeanice Falls, eds. Russellville, AR: n.p., 1988.

Murdoch, Katie. "William L. McElwee," in *History of Pope County, Arkansas* (Winston-Salem, NC: Hunter Publishing Co., 1979), 339–40.

Oates, Calvin Grier. "Biographical Sketch of John Oates, Sr., and Family." Unpublished typescript, copy in author's file provided by Tamara Tidwell.

Oates, Franklin Knox. "Early History of the Oates and Related Families." Unpublished typescript, copy in author's file.

Oates, Monroe. "History of Pisgah Church, Arkansas," *Associate Reformed Presbyterian,* May 6, 1884.

———. "A Sketch of Thirty Years of a Pastor's Life," *Associate Reformed Presbyterian,* January 12, 1898.

———. "Mr. A. N. Falls," *Associate Reformed Presbyterian,* undated [1900] clipping. Copy in author's file.

Oates, Thomas M., to A. Wier and Family, March 9, 1854. Copy in author's file provided by Mrs. Moffatt Ware.

Oates, Wade. Interview, Pottsville, Arkansas, October 14, 1985.

Parker, Carl F. "Analysis of Certain Transactions Recorded in Journal of Parker's Mills, Galley Creek, Pope County, Arkansas as They Relate to Life and History of Persons Involved," *Pope County Historical Association Quarterly,* 12 (December 1977), 45–49.

———. "James Whitesides," enclosed in Parker to Mrs. Ollen Kay, November 2, 1978. Copy in author's file.

———. "The Parker Family History," in *History of Pope County, Arkansas* (Winston-Salem, NC: Hunter Publishing Co., 1979), 367–68.

Patterson, Dorcas Ferguson, and Alice Ann Harris. "The Ferguson Family History," in *History of Pope County, Arkansas* (Winston-Salem, NC: Hunter Publishing Co., 1979), 224.

———. "The Henry Family History" in *History of Pope County, Arkansas* (Winston-Salem, NC: Hunter Publishing Co., 1979), 260–61.

"Pisgah-Bethany-Pottsville Associate Reformed Presbyterian Church of Pottsville, Pope County, Arkansas." 1978. Unpublished typescript, copy in author's file.

"Pope County Company 'B,'" in *History of Pope County, Arkansas* (Topeka, KS: Josten's Publishing Co., 1981), 56–57.

Pope County Deed Records.

Pope County Tax Records.

Pope County Will Records.

Rice, Nina Daniels. "The Daniels Family." Unpublished typescript, copy in author's file.

Rogers, Lora Beth Henry. "Arkansas Covered Wagon Pioneers: The Hughey Family." 1989. Unpublished typescript, copy in author's file.

————. "The History and Genealogy of the James A. Bradley Family: Members of the Covered Wagon Families Who Settled in Arkansas." 1994. Unpublished typescript, copy in author's file provided by Lora Beth Henry Rogers.

Rogers, Lora Beth Henry, to W. O. Ragsdale, July 17, 1991. Copy in author's file.

Scott, Hannah Haw Lewis. "The Anthony Family," in *History of Pope County, Arkansas* (Topeka, KS: Josten's Publishing Co., 1981), 212–13.

Scott Family Letters. In private collection of Mrs. Embry Scott Shoemaker, who provided access for the author. Excerpts from these letters appeared in Viva Mae Moore, ed., "Early History from Old Letters," *Pope County Historical Association Quarterly*, 5 (December 1970): 24–31.

Simmons, Mrs. William (Mae Dell Brown), comp. "Genealogy of Hollinger Daniel Brown, Jr., and Allied Families." Unpublished typescript, copy in author's file provided by Mary Elizabeth Henry Kroencke.

Sinclair, E. B. "Gregory Sinclair," in *History of Pope County, Arkansas* (Winston-Salem, NC: Hunter Publishing Co., 1979), 421–22.

Sinclair, Thomas G. "Samuel Sinclair," in *Wayne County, Tennessee, 1817–1995: History and Families* (Paducah, KY: Turner Publishing Co., 1995), 379–80.

Stevenson, J. W. *God in My Unbelief* (New York and Evanston: Harper & Row). This account of Stevenson's first pastorate in Crainie, in the Scots Highlands, was background inspiration in writing about the Pisgah Church.

Stevenson, R. M. *Studies in Our Church History.* Due West, SC: Associate Reformed Presbyterian Co., 1916.

Stroud, John C. "Gally Rock Men Who Fought for the Confederacy," in *History of Pope County, Arkansas* (Topeka, KS: Josten's Publishing Co., 1981), 55.

Tucker, S. C., Jr. "Crow Mountain Volunteers," *Pope County Historical Association Quarterly*, 4 (June 1970): 86–88.

————. *To Sell a Good Bull: A Story of the Arkansas River Valley.* Dardanelle, AR: Author, 1976.

U.S. Agricultural Census, 1860, 1870, Pope County, Arkansas.

U.S. Census, Population Schedules, 1850, 1860, 1870, Pope County, Arkansas.

U.S. Census, Slave Schedules, 1850, Gaston County, North Carolina.

U.S. Census, Slave Schedules, 1850, York County, North Carolina.

U.S. Census, Slave Schedules, 1860, Pope County, Arkansas.

*Weekly Tribune* (Russellville, AR), 1936.

Weir, Alexander, to James Bradley, January 11, 1859. Copy in author's file, provided by Lora Beth Henry Rogers.

Wharton, Ruth Bell. "Alexander Bell," in *History of Pope County, Arkansas* (Winston-Salem, NC: Hunter Publishing Co., 1979), 145.

———. "Alexander Dickey, Sr." Unpublished typescript, copy in author's file provided by Ruth Bell Wharton.

———. "Alexander Kidd Dickey," in *History of Pope County, Arkansas* (Winston-Salem, NC: Hunter Publishing Co., 1979), 213–14.

Williamson, Mrs. Marvin, and Neill H. Bell. "The Oates Family,"*Arkansas Valley Historical Papers,* No. 29 (June 1954), 1–9.

Willson, John, to Alexander Wear, April 25, 1842. Copy in author's file provided by Mrs. Moffatt Ware.

Wilson, Moses, to Alexander Wear, April 30, 1842. Copy in author's file provided by Mrs. Moffatt Ware.

# Index

Corinth, Miss., 77
Corn, 47
Cotton, 48, 49–50, 100, 104
County Tyrone, Ireland, 33
Cove Cemetery, 21
Covenanters, 6–7, 22
Crawford, James, 10
Crawford, William, 10
Cree, Rev. John, 10
Crops, 46–50, 89, 103, 104
Crowder's Creek, N.C., 3
Crowder's Mountain, N.C., 3
Crow Mountain, Ark., 2, 30, 46, 79, 88, 108

Daniels, Amanda P., 64
Daniels, Jasper N., 64
Daniels, Margaret E., 64
Daniels, Mary Ann Blackwood, 64
Dardanelle, Ark., 49, 78, 79
Dare, Thomas J., 15
Davis, Caleb, 76, 80
Davis, Johnathan, 68
Decatur, Ga., 18, 32
Des Arc, Ark., 14
Dickey, Alexander Kidd, 31, 32, 34, 35, 36, 46, 58, 66, 69, 98
Dickey, Andrew J., 58
Dickey, Elizabeth, 58
Dickey, Elizabeth J., 58
Dickey, James, 53–54, 57, 58, 76
Dickey, Jannice (Jenny) Sinclair, 32, 33, 35
Dickey, John Oates, 58, 75, 77
Dickey, Margaret, 58
Dickey, Margaret Blackwood, 58
Dickey, Mary, 58
Dickey, Mary McGill Oates, 58
Dickey, Mary Oates, 77

Dickey, Nancy, 49, 52
Dickey, R. H., 97
Dickey, Robert H., 76
Dickey, Samuel B., 58, 77, 97–98
Dickey, William, 58
Dickey, William B., 46, 83
Dickson, J. A., 69
Diet, 52
Dixon, Rev. William, 10
Dodson, E. W., 95
Dover, Ark., 15, 44, 45
Due West, S.C., 17, 23, 28, 67
Dunn, James, 10
Drew County, Ark., 40, 67

Ebenezer Associate Reformed Church, Va., 102
Elders, 24, 25, 66
*Elizabeth*, 33
Elliott, Robert, 10
Ellis County, Tex., 85, 88
Emancipation Proclamation, 78
Embry, Ben T., 53–54, 73, 75–76, 92
Erskine, Ebenezer, 6
Erskine, Rev. Ralph, 6
Erskine College, 17, 23, 28, 67, 68, 102
Erskine Theological Seminary, 18, 102
Ewing, Cyrus C., 49, 51, 72, 81, 86, 94–95, 96
Ewing, DeWitt, 94, 95
Ewing, Elizabeth, 94
Ewing, Hale, 94
Ewing, Missouri, 72–73
Ewing, Winter, 81, 94

Falls, Andrew Nael, 13, 17, 24, 26, 30, 40, 44, 45, 51, 54, 65, 86, 89, 91, 104; as slaveholder, 18, 48; land bought by, 19, 46; elegy by, 21; letter of, 21–22,

26, 27–28; as community builder, 27–28, 29–30; as elder, 36, 66, 69, 98

at, 43–44, 46, 53–54; crops at, 46–
47; self-sufficiency at, 52–53;
literacy at, 54; slavery issue at, 73;
Union sentiment at, 74, 75, 81–82;
captured troops from, 76; war casualties from, 76, 80–81, 89–90;
refugees from, 85, 86, 91; women at,
87–88; soldiers return to, 91–92;
devastation at, 82–83, 90–91, 93;
privation at, 88–89, 93–95, 96; sectional animosities at, 95, 96; postwar economy of, 96, 100, 103–5;
descendants from, 107–8
Pisgah, N.C., 1, 2, 3, 8, 13, 17, 20, 29,
57, 73
Pisgah Cemetery, 43, 108
Pisgah Church, Ark., 24; organization of,
24–25, 27; elders at, 25, 36, 97, 98;
erection of, 30; ministers for, 36,
40–41, 67–68, 99; Communion
Service at, 40; membership of, 67,
68–69, 106, 107; prosperity of, 68–
69; problems within, 96–97, 98, 99,
105, 106; decline of, 105–6; historical importance of, 107
Pisgah Church, N.C., 3, 5, 10, 11, 16, 18,
34, 58, 59, 60, 64, 74
Pleasant Grove Church, Ga., 102
Pope County, Ark., 1, 2; crops in, 2, 3–4,
21, 31; roads to, 14, 15; population
of, 14, 53, 57; health conditions in,
15, 31; land in, 32, 43–44, 64, 66;
migrations from, 45; transportation
in, 51; diet in, 51–52; literacy in, 54;
secession debate in, 67–68; warfare
in, 79, 85–86; political violence in,
95–96
Potts, Kirkbride, 44
Potts Station, 100, 106
Pottsville, Ark., 1, 11, 15, 30
Pottsville Church, 106
Prairie County, Ark., 19, 32
Prairie de Ann, Ark., 79

Presbytery of New York, 8
Prosperity Church, Ark., 40, 68, 100, 105
Psalms, 7, 9, 97

Quigg, Rev. Henry, 97
Quinn, Ann Falls, 18, 86
Quinn, Isabella McArthur, 63, 76
Quinn, James, 18, 24, 83, 86; land
bought by, 19, 46; as elder, 25, 66,
69, 98
Quinn, John, 76
Quinn, John W., 63
Quinn, Mary, 76
Quinn, Robert, 63, 76, 83
Quinn, Sarepta N., 63, 76

Railroads, 31–32, 50–51
Randall, Capt. John, 76
Rankin, W. H., 44
Rankin, William W., 15
Raymond, Catherine, 61
Raymond, Dr. Franklin R., 53, 60, 61,
63, 67, 69, 98
Raymond, Griselda, 61
Raymond, Jennette, 61
Rea, Francis, 10
Reed, Eliza, 90
Reformed Presbyterian Church, 6, 7–8
Reformed Presbyterian Presbytery, 8
Remove, Ark., 14
Revolutionary War, 9, 59
Rhine (slave), 35
Rice, C., 49
Richmond, Ky., 78
Riverboats, 20, 34–35, 49–50, 61
Roads, 14, 18–19, 20, 61
Robinson, Samuel M., 5
Rock Roe Lake, Ark., 20
Rome, Ga., 18, 32